THE CLEOBURY MORTIMER AND DITTON PRIORS LIGHT RAILWAY

THE LIGHT RAILWAYS ACT, 1896.

Cleobury Mortimer and Ditton Priors

LIGHT RAILWAY.

ORDER OF THE LIGHT RAILWAY COMMISSIONERS

Authorising the construction of a Light Railway between Cleobury Mortimer and Ditton Priors, both in the County of Salop.

PRELIMINARY.

Short Title.   **1.** This Order may be cited as "THE CLEOBURY MORTIMER AND DITTON PRIORS LIGHT RAILWAY ORDER, 1900" and shall come into force on the date on which it is confirmed by the Board of Trade and that date is hereinafter referred to as "the commencement of this Order."

Interpretation.   **2.** Words and expressions to which by the principal Act or any Acts in whole or in part incorporated with this Order meanings are assigned have in this Order (unless the context otherwise requires) the same respective meanings and in this Order—

An extract from the Cleobury Mortimer and Ditton Priors Light Railway Order of 1900.

THE CLEOBURY MORTIMER AND DITTON PRIORS LIGHT RAILWAY

by W. Smith and K. Beddoes

Oxford Publishing Co.

ACKNOWLEDGEMENTS

W. Atkinson, R. Carpenter, B. Crowther, T. Davies, C. Eyre, D. Fraser, Mrs. M. Howells, J. Lawley, B. Moone, E. Mountford, E. Tonks, E. and T. Wall, W. Watkiss. Lord Boyne's Estate Office, British Rail Archives, *Bridgnorth Journal*, Department of the Environment, members of the H.M.R.S., members of the I.R.S., Kidderminster Library, Lacon Childe School pupils past and present, National Railway Museum, York, Shropshire County Records Office and Library, Stottesdon Parish Council, *Tenbury Advertiser*. The following railwaymen: J. Bacon, R. Davies, the late E. Hitchen, N. Howe, the late F. Harvey (and Mrs. Harvey), C. Robinson, L. Shingles. The following quarry personnel: B. and C. Bowen, H. Bradley, W. and A. Caines, A. and E. Cartwright, M. Childs, C. Cooper, D. Glaze, J. Lewis, J. Parker, A. Ritchie, W. Wroe, Mr. and Mrs. Hall, Mr. Morris, J. G. Brennan, G. T. V. Stacey, and L.C.G.B., Cyril Trigg.

BIBLIOGRAPHY

GWR Coaches, Harris, David & Charles
History of the Great Western Railway, MacDermott and Clinker, Ian Allan
Industrial Locomotives, Handbook G, Industrial Railway Society
Light Railways, W. J. Davies, Ian Allan
Locomotives of the GWR, R.C.T.S.
A Pictorial Record of Great Western Coaches, J. Russell, O.P.C.
The GWR Magazine, 1938
Historical Metallurgy Bulletin, N. Mutton, January 1966
The Locomotive Magazine, June 1921
Railway Magazine, 1897, 1909, 1938
Railway Observer

Printed by B.H. Blackwell in the City of Oxford
Set by Getset at Eynsham
Bound by Kemp Hall Bindery, Oxford

Published by:
Oxford Publishing Company
8 The Roundway
Headington
Oxford

CONTENTS

The Ditton Priors branch platform at Cleobury Mortimer Junction in 1938, showing 0-6-0PT No. 28.

R.K. Cope

FOREWORD

THE Cleobury Mortimer and Ditton Priors Light Railway was built at the beginning of this century to assist quarrying on the Brown Clee Hill and to improve transport in the Rea Valley for the farming folk who lived in that somewhat remote district.

My family, who owned a large proportion of the land at the line's northern extremity, were amongst the promoters and my Great Grandfather and his son, The Hon. Eustace Hamilton-Russell, were enthusiastic and active in its promotion and establishment.

My memories of the line stretch back only to the days when goods were carried, just prior to the Second World War. As a child I remember the fascination of watching the cable railway to the quarry, and the loads being lowered to the valley below. The war came and we all gathered scrap metal for melting to make munitions. The Incline Railway had closed and many happy hours as a child were spent picking up nuts and bolts from the track, the rails already having gone, and pieces of old cable, some of which can still be found today embedded in the grass beside the track.

The Cleobury Mortimer and Ditton Priors Railway had its chance to play a part in the war effort and, as a munitions carrier, its speed limit was lowered to walking pace. This of course gave the crew time to dismount and set snares. The following day they could be seen jumping down to collect their harvest of rabbits!

It was a sad but inevitable day when the line finally closed. This excellent record of its life is a very valuable addition to the history of railways in this country, and particularly valuable as a memorial to a railway which for several decades served this part of Shropshire well.

Boyne

(The Rt. Hon. The Viscount Boyne.)

PREFACE

FOR such a rural county, Salop is surprisingly rich in industrial archaeology. We have attempted in this book to present a fragment of this in the history of one of the county's better known railway branch lines. In this case the story of the railway is inextricably bound up with the dhustone quarrying industry of the Brown Clee Hill. It has been our aim to state the facts as we understand them to-day, possibly to stimulate further research and interest or perhaps to recall and record one facet of life in the region.

We have been extremely fortunate in receiving help from many directions and wish to clearly acknowledge the participation of many local residents who have willingly given assistance. The line was a late arrival on the railway map of Great Britain which has made it possible to trace men and women today whose memories reach back to the earliest days of the line and of the quarries.

The railway has been well documented photographically and we have had access to three important collections. The first collection was made available by Mr William Atkinson and dates from the days when his father was consultant engineer to the contractors Bott & Stennett; secondly those of the late R.K. Cope who photographed the whole line with loving attention in the 1930's have been made available and finally Geoff Bannister's superbly evocative pictures made in the early BR period complete the photographic record. In Ditton Priors there are men like Charlie Cooper and Cliff Bowen now in their eighties but with vivid memories of life in the quarries before the

First World War, working for 2d (1p) per hour breaking stone 10 hours per day. Also still living in Ditton is Archie Cartwright, one time driver of the small quarry 0-6-0 locos, and Harold Bradley driver of the 2ft gauge "Whizz-Bangs". Mr Alec Ritchie of Kidderminster gave valuable information about the plant especially the tar plant and machinery.

Ben Crowther has provided a meticulous description of the working and maintenance of the Detton Ford aerial ropeway and Ernie Wall of Oreton has given much background information to this study.

Like all railway historians we are indebted to the access afforded to official records at the Public Record Office and to the cumulative information from many learned enthusiasts of the various railway societies who have readily answered our questions.

Returning to the Salop area again we are keen to acknowledge the assistance freely given by the Salop C.R.O. and the staff at the *Bridgnorth Journal* office.

Dick Riley has given us much help, advice and encouragement but such is the large total of acknowledgements that we wish to make, we set out a list in the sincerest hope that we have not excluded any of our helpers but finally we offer our thanks to Frank Johnson, who has superbly prepared prints and photographs of all ages and conditions, and to our typist Mrs Vera Griffiths.

W. Smith and K. Beddoes
Cleobury Mortimer
1980

Opposite page Cleobury, Manning Wardle 0-6-0ST No. 1735, at Cleobury Town in 1908.

Real Photographs

THE C.M. & D.P. ROUTE

● **Ditton Priors Halt**

● **Cleobury North Crossing**

Brown Clee Hill

● **Burwarton Halt**

● **Aston Botterell Siding**

● **Stottesdon Halt**

● **Prescott Siding** (4)

● **Detton Ford Siding** (3)

Planned to be known as:—
1—Cleobury Mortimer
2—Neen Savage
3—Detton Mill
4—Oreton

Titterstone Clee Hill

● **Chilton Siding** (2)

R. Rea

● **Cleobury Town Halt** (1)

To Bewdley

● **Cleobury Mortimer**

To Tenbury Wells

Scale
—————
1 mile

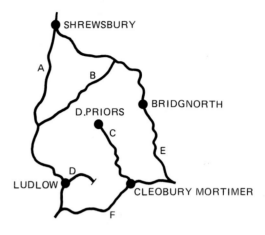

THE RAILWAYS OF S.E. SHROPSHIRE *c.1930*

● SHREWSBURY

A

B

D.PRIORS

BRIDGNORTH

C

E

D

LUDLOW

CLEOBURY MORTIMER

F

A—"North and West" line—*L.M.S./G.W.*
B—Much Wenlock branch—*G.W.R.*
C—C.M. & D.P. branch—*G.W.R.*
D—Clee Hill mineral branch—*L.M.S./G.W.*
E—Severn Valley branch—*G.W.R.*
F—Tenbury & Bewdley branch—*G.W.R.*

CHAPTER ONE

The Background

THE area of Salop through which this railway ran is part of the region in the south-east corner of the county which can be defined as the South Shropshire Hills. Here the two Clee Hills, the Titterstone Clee and the Brown Clee, form the highest land in the whole of the county, and are dominant basalt capped hills within a landscape where today, the isolated farm and scattered hamlet are still more common than the nucleated village.

Although the view is one of a rolling, agricultural, well wooded piece of countryside, the region has in fact had a long history of industrial involvement. Economic minerals occur here: coal, iron, limestone, dhustone, (basalt) and some copper lie beneath the farmland or the open common land of the Clees. The history of industrial activity reaches back into the sixteenth century, when a tiny, embryonic industrial revolution based on the charcoal-fuelled blast furnace enabled iron to be produced at Cleobury Mortimer as early as the 1560s. A small blast furnace at Abdon was known to be operating a hundred years later and, again, a century later a furnace was operating at Charlcotte on the Cleobury Brook, a tributary of the River Rea. Local iron forges existed at the end of the eighteenth century on the River Rea at Hardwick, Prescott and the Lower and Upper forges at Cleobury Mortimer. At this time, not very far away, waggons were already rattling over iron rails in Coalbrookdale and the early eighteenth century Shropshire inspired industrialization had commenced its world shattering effect. The extracting industries of the Brown Clee Hill had no waggonways or advanced transport of any kind, therefore one of the big problems in mining and quarrying was how to get the coal and ironstone down the steep slopes of the Clee to the customers below the hill and further afield. There was no regular road to the summit of the Brown Clee until the mid nineteenth century, not even a cart track, so pack horse and the backs of men (and sometimes their wives' backs also) were the only means of haulage off the mines. It was during the nineteenth century that stone quarrying gradually replaced coal and iron mining on the Brown Clee.

Thomas Telford, Shropshire County Surveyor in the late eighteenth century, knew and prized the good quality of the dhustone basalt which caps both the Clee Hills and by the late nineteenth century the stone had become much sought after as a strong road surfacing material and as setts for the construction of numerous tramways springing up in the expanding towns of late Victorian Britain. The growing trade in dhustone had been the stimulus for the construction of the heavily graded railway between Ludlow and Titterstone Clee Hill summit from a junction on the old Shrewsbury and Hereford line. This mineral line began operation in 1864 only eleven days later than a line was opened by the GWR passing across the Southern end of the Rea Valley at Cleobury Mortimer connecting Bewdley with Tenbury and the LNWR/GW joint line at Woofferton Junction.

The Rea Valley of Shropshire was, by the end of the nineteenth century, inside a triangle of railways with Shrewsbury at the apex, and the Severn Valley line to the east carrying away coal from the Wyre Forest Coalfield into the Midlands.

The Shrewsbury and Hereford Railway "North and West" route ran on the western side and the Tenbury-Bewdley line lay to the south. Cutting across the triangle to the north of the Rea valley was the Much Wenlock branch. Transport for the many farmers in the Rea Valley to and from the local livestock markets at Kidderminster, Tenbury Wells and Cleobury Mortimer was not convenient and the easing of this situation coupled with the opportunity of getting rail access to the Brown Clee dhustone sparked the idea to make a quarry railhead at Ditton Priors and link it to Cleobury Mortimer, on the Great Western Railway, bringing into being the line known as the Cleobury Mortimer and Ditton Priors Light Railway. The plan, no doubt, became possible as a result of the 1896 Light Railway Act which altered the legal restrictions of existing Railway Acts so as to make it easier to build rural railways.

For the purpose of making and maintaining the railway and for the other purposes a company known as the "Cleobury Mortimer and Ditton Prior Light Railway Company" was formed. There were to be five directors which could be varied by the Company down to three or up to seven, and the qualification of directors was that they must be in possession, in their own right, of not less than two hundred and fifty pounds in the share capital of the Company.

Following support from various informal meetings held in early 1900, Mr Everard Calthrop was engaged to survey and draw up plans and sections of the proposed route.

In May 1900 an application was duly made to the Light Railway Commissioners by Viscount Boyne and Admiral Robert Woodward in pursuance of the Light Railways Act 1896 for an Order to authorise the construction of the Light Railway. A public enquiry was held in October 1900 at the Oddfellows Hall, Cleobury Mortimer by the Earl of Jersey and Colonel Boughey, Board of Trade Light Railway Commissioners, as to the expendiency of granting the application. The counsel for the promoters explained that there was practically no opposition from public bodies or landowners and expressed regret, that on account of cost, the railway could not be constructed nearer the centre of Cleobury Mortimer. The Engineer then explained the scheme in detail. Mr Williamson of Kinlet, Mr Dodgson, agent to Lord Boyne, Mr Howells of Wheathill Court, Mr Boyle, Land Agent of Middleton, Mr Doolittle, Estate Agent of Bewdley, Lord Boyne, Admiral Woodward and Mr Davis, Chairman of Cleobury Mortimer District Council all signified to the Commissioners that they were in favour of the scheme. Mr G. Lloyd-Baker, a land owner at Neen Savage was the only voice heard against the scheme as he felt it could inconvenience his tenantry without giving them any advantages. Another feeling of the meeting, expressed by Mr Davis, was that because of the distance of the station on the Bridgnorth road from the centre of Cleobury Mortimer, the railway should be asked to provide free delivery to and from the centre. The meeting closed with the Commissioners intimating that they could report favourably on the scheme. Soon after this meeting the application was granted with the title "The Cleobury Mortimer and Ditton Priors Light Railway Order 1900" and it was to come into force on the date on which it was confirmed by the Board of Trade.

Ungated level crossing at Neen Savage, showing original flat bottom track. 24th September, 1938.

R.K. Cope

The Authorisation gave the Company the power to make and maintain the railway subject to the provisions of the Order according to the levels and lines shown on the Plan and Section. The Authorisation states that the railway is:

12 Miles 1 Furlong 7 chains or thereabouts in length wholly situate in the County of Salop, commencing in the parish of Cleobury Mortimer by junction with GWR (Tenbury and Bewdley branch) at the point 26 chains measured Southward along the said Railway from the Booking office at Cleobury Mortimer station, running in a Northerly direction across the main road from Bewdley to Cleobury Mortimer thence in a North-Westerly direction keeping on the North-Eastern side of Cleobury Mortimer and Neen Savage and up the valley of the River Rea in a Northerly direction past Detton Mill and Oreton to Stottesden (spelt in this way by the railway at that time). Thence in a North Westerly direction past Aston Botterell, Burwarton, Cleobury North and terminating in the parish of Ditton Priors at the point 440 yards or thereabouts measured in an Easterly direction from the "Howard Arms" Hotel along the main road from Ditton Priors to Bridgnorth. The railway shall be constructed on a gauge of four feet eight and a half inches and the motive power shall be steam or such other motive power as the Board of Trade may approve.

Subject to the provisions of the Order the Company was given the power to take and use the lands shown on the Plan and described in the Book of Reference. The Book of Reference shows the considerable amount of land already available to the Company from the Boyne Estate.

The powers of the Company for compulsory purchase were to cease after three years from the commencement of the Order and there was to be a restriction on taking houses occupied by the labouring class. The labouring class means according to the Order:

mechanics, artisans, labourers and others working for wages. Hawkers, costermongers, persons not working for wages at some trade or handicraft without employing others, except members of their families, and persons other than domestic servants, whose income does not exceed an average of thirty shillings a week, and the families of any such persons who may be residing with them.

The period for completion of the works was within five years from the commencement of the Order or such extended time as the Board of Trade approved. Power to deviate from the lines and levels of the railway as delineated on the Plan and Section were given subject to several restrictions notably that no curve radius be reduced to less than nine chains, nor any gradient made steeper than 1:50 without the consent of the Board of Trade. The Company was required to carry the railway over the public road (No 7 on the plan, the Cleobury Mortimer-Bewdley road) by means of a single span bridge being not less than forty feet span and eighteen feet high having a clear headway above the surface of the road for the space of ten feet over the road with a clear height at the springing of the arch not less than twelve feet above the surface of the road on the level. As to crossing roads on the level the Company was required to erect and maintain gates across the railway on each side of the road in the parish of Neen Savage and in the parish of Cleobury North (numbered 20A on the plan).

Provision was made for the additional gates on other level crossings should either the Company or the Board of Trade require. On the two roads which were gated the Company was to employ "a proper person to open and close such gates on either side of the level crossing". The gates had to be constantly closed across the railway at all times when the road was not being crossed by a train. As to level crossings without gates, the Company was required to construct cattle guards at each end of the road to prevent animals entering the railway. Three hundred yards from an ungated crossing it was stipulated that there should be a five foot post with a special speed limit figure clearly visible to an engine driver. The Company had also to place warning boards for the public on the road approach to the ungated crossings at points fifty yards on either side of the line. The Order required the Company to make good all damage to any public road wherever a crossing was made, and to maintain and repair such a road for twelve months following the completion of the line. After this the Company was to be responsible for the road between the rails and a width of seven feet outside the rails on each side of the railway.

Provisions were made in the Order to deal with the junction to be made with the Great Western Railway's Tenbury and Bewdley line at Cleobury Mortimer, and the manner and form of the junctions had to be approved by the Great Western Railway Company. The CM & DP Light Railway were to provide, to the satisfaction of the Great Western Company, "all necessary stations, sidings and works for the proper and convenient accommodation and interchange of traffic passing between the railway and the Great Western Railway". Any alterations or re-arrangement of platforms, lines or sidings belonging to the Great Western which were required to accommodate the new Company at Cleobury Mortimer had to be paid for by the CM & DP Light Railway Company.

The railway was due to cross the pipe-line of Birmingham's water supply and the Order protected the Corporation in so much as one month before construction of any part of the railway in the parish of Neen Savage the Company had to give notice of any works liable to affect the line of the aqueduct authorised by the Birmingham Corporation Water Act 1892. The Company had to make and maintain two subways, each fifteen feet wide, for the purpose of carrying the water pipe line under the railway, and constructed to the reasonable approval of Birmingham Corporation. The Corporation's engineers and workers were given the liberty, under the Order, "to enter upon, pass and re-pass, over and across the railway (but at their own risk in all respects, and so as not to create any interference with the traffic of the railway) at the point where the same passes over the subways".

As to working the line the Company was restricted by the Order to use no vehicle bringing a greater weight than twelve tons upon any one pair of wheels, or if the rails weighed not less than sixty pounds per yard the weight allowed could rise to four-teen tons per axle. The Board of Trade were to consent in writing before the Company could operate anything heavier. In this section of the Order, the speed limit was laid down as 25 mph except when passing over a gradient steeper than 1 in 50 when the limit was set at 20 mph, and when a train or engine was passing over any curve the radius of which is less than nine chains it was not to exceed 10 mph. Approaching ungated road crossings, the speed at the 300 yards distance was to be no more than 10 mph, but with a rider that the Board of Trade may fix a lower maximum "if the view of the railway from the road near the crossing is at any point or for any distance so obstructed to render the higher maximum speed unsafe for the public using the road". Also the Company was not allowed to let any vehicle stand unnecessarily across a level crossing.

If the motive power used upon the railway was to be a mechanical power other than steam or electric, the Order stipulated that the consent of, and approval of the Board of Trade must first be sought. Further special provisions were written down in case the Company decided on electric traction and amongst several safety precautions was that the Company had to employ insulated returns or uninsulated returns of low resistance if the case arose.

The Order set out the rates for merchandise charges for small parcel and maximum rates for passengers which was 3d (1½p) per mile for 1st class, 2d (1p) per mile 2nd class and 1d (½p) per mile 3rd class.

The capital was laid down to be £96,000 in shares of £1 each. The Great Western Railway were given power to subscribe any sum which they thought fit having first been given authority by three quarters of their shareholders at a general meeting of the GWR Company. The Company was given power to borrow sum or sums of money not exceeding £32,000. The Light Railway Commissioners stated that the rails must weigh at least fifty six pounds per yard, and on curves with radii of less than nine chains a check rail was to be provided. If flat bottom rails and wooden sleepers were to be used,

> (a) The rails at the joints shall be secured to the sleepers by fang through-bolts or by coach-screws or by double spikes on the outside of the rail with a bearing plate and (b) the rails on curves with radii of less than nine chains shall be tied to gauge iron or steel ties at suitable intervals or in such other manner as may be approved by the Board of Trade.

It was stated by the Commissioners, that turntables need not be provided but no tender-engine could be run tender foremost at a rate of speed exceeding 15 mph. The Commissioners made it clear that signals were to be erected if the system of working entailed trains crossing or passing one another at any point; home signals at the entrance points of such a crossing point and distance signals (*sic*) if a home signal was not visible from a quarter of a mile away, but the line was never signalled apart from the running lines in Cleobury Mortimer station and the approach off the branch into Cleobury Mortimer.

Finally the Commissioners refer to platforms which "shall be provided to the satisfaction of the Board of Trade unless all carriages in use on the railway are constructed with proper and convenient means of access to and from the same to the level of the ground of the rail". Here it was laid down that there was no obligation on the Company to "provide shelter or conveniences at any station or stopping place."

Wilson steam navvy excavating the cutting at 1m 25c in 1907.

W. Atkinson

CHAPTER TWO

The Beginning

THE Light Railway Order under section 10 of the Light Railway was granted on 23rd March, 1901 and empowered the Company and the GWR to enter into agreements with one another. Stations or halts were to be provided "with suitable access" at Neen Savage, Detton Mill, Oreton, Aston Botterell and Ditton Priors. At a meeting on 21st April, 1901 the Board of Directors was officially appointed and it was the original intention of the directors of the Light Railway to negotiate for the Great Western Railway to work the line. They approached Lord Boyne in the early summer of 1901 with a view to him subscribing capital in order to strengthen the financial position of the Company in its dealings with the GWR. Then hopefully, having won over the Great Western, the directors could happily apply to the general public for the balance of the subscription.

In June 1901 a letter was sent signed by the CM & DP Lt Rly Secretary, Mr J. Polglasse, to the legal Manager of the GWR, Paddington, informing him of the incorporation of the CM & DP Lt Rly, by Light Railway Order, to construct and work the line 12¼ miles long from Cleobury Mortimer, Great Western Railway Station, to Ditton Priors. It was stated that the capital authorised by the Order was £96,000 with power to borrow, on mortgage another £32,000 and that capital cost of the undertaking was estimated at £88,048.

Information was given concerning the Board of Directors. The Chairman was then Sir Alexander Wilson Kt, Chairman of the Mercantile Bank of India, Director of the Barsi Light Railway, the Bengal and Assam Railway and the Nilgiri Railway. The appointed Engineer was Mr Everard Calthrop who had worked under Sir Alexander Wilson's directorship during the construction of the Barsi Light Railway. The director nominated by Rt Hon. Viscount Boyne was his son, The Hon. A. Hamilton Russell and R. Caryl Roberts of the Manor House, Cleobury Mortimer was the nominee of Admiral Woodward.

Several documents were sent to the GWR including a statement dealing with the agricultural and mining development of the region which could be expected to follow the construction of the railway. Two geological reports were sent. One by Mr Arthur C. Auden, Mining engineer of Bewdley, on the dhustone rock of the Brown Clee Hill and one on the Chorley and Kinlet Coal Royalties by Mr Noel T. Beech, Mining Engineer of Newport, Mon. Finally a request was made for the GWR to receive a deputation of one or more of the directors, accompanied by Mr Calthrop, with a view to discussing terms for the working of the undertaking by the GWR when the line had been constructed.

The Great Western Railway must have already been familiar with the nature of the dhustone basalt from the rock that they moved down the GWR/LNWR joint line off the neighbouring Titterstone Clee to Ludlow, but Mr Auden, in his report, was keen to point out the better quality of the Brown Clee sample.

In its formation, the crystallization of the Brown Clee Basalt, he stated, appeared to be slightly different from that of the Titterstone Basalt in that the microliths were at a shade greater angle to the cleavage in the Brown Clee example. This meant that the surface of the Brown Clee stone would not become so quickly polished and slippery when used to surface a road.

Mr Auden did not foresee any great difficulty in working the Brown Clee outcrop except on the western side where the deep pitch of the strata would make top work essential at first as undercut work would be risky because of rock falls. As the working face was approximately circular in plan, Mr Auden suggested that a double track narrow gauge line might circle the crown of the hill, and several old coal shafts on the top of Abdon Clee could be reopened to provide boiler fuel.

Mr Auden foresaw some opposition to a gravity ropeway but was doubtful about the economics of an alternative aerial ropeway which, he felt, would have a heavy cost in upkeep, and be liable to serious loss through breakdown particularly if the problem occurred in the course of a night shift. The stone crusher station, he felt, should be situated beside the railway line in Ditton Priors with storage bins there as well as bins over the track, so that shortage of available wagons would not occur as it could do with direct stone loading alone. Tramway setts were in great demand at this time, and it was Mr Auden's opinion that production should concentrate on this item in preference to road metal which could be sold as a by-product from sett manufacture.

A warm, well lighted shed should be built for sett makers at Ditton Priors so that they might continue work in winter from stock accumulated during double quarrying shifts in the long daylight hours of summer. Mr Auden suggested the eventual use of a sett making machine, but only when sufficiently large quantities of stock had been built up so that any consequent strike of hand makers following the introduction of machinery would not result in loss of trade. The question of labour at Ditton Priors needed considering, and Mr Auden suggested the building of cottages near the work but these to be kept the absolute property of the Quarry Company, as "men will think twice before striking and giving trouble when notice to quit them will be given to them as a consequence".

To the east of the proposed line lay the Wyre Forest Coalfield whose products were already being transported via the Great Western's Severn Valley line through Highley. The western end of the coalfield adjoined the Cleobury Mortimer and Ditton Priors line near Stottesdon under the Kinlet and Chorley Estate. Mr Beech, in his report, wrote favourably on the availability of valuable coal and iron seams which could be developed as a result of railway access.

The report went on to describe the economic mineral resources that could be tapped after the railway had been built. The line was planned to pass by Oreton where the excellent carboniferous limestone was already being quarried. Another, different stone, had been used in building Burwarton Rectory, and was quarried near the line at the Birches. Near the Farlow road and at Prescott was good sharp sand, and clay for brick making was available near Cleobury North and Ditton Priors.

The GWR's reply did not share local enthusiasm for the line, and further requests were consequently sent out for a meeting with Mr J. Wilkinson, General Manager of the GWR, in order to try to convince the powers at Paddington that this was not just another piece of railway speculation.

Eventually, in the autumn of 1901, the Great Western came up with some definite suggestions. They were willing to work the line for 2/- (10p) per train mile with a minimum of five trains

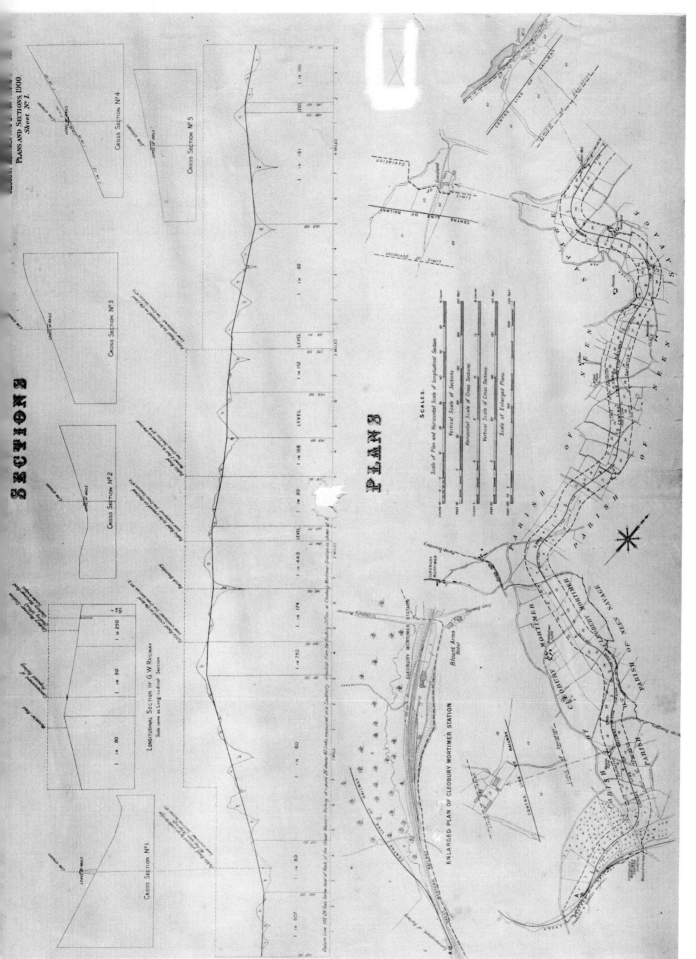

Plans and sections of the Cleobury Mortimer & Ditton Priors Light Railway.
Courtesy Stottesdon Parish Council

Plans and sections of the Cleobury Mortimer & Ditton Priors Light Railway.
Courtesy Stottesdon Parish Council

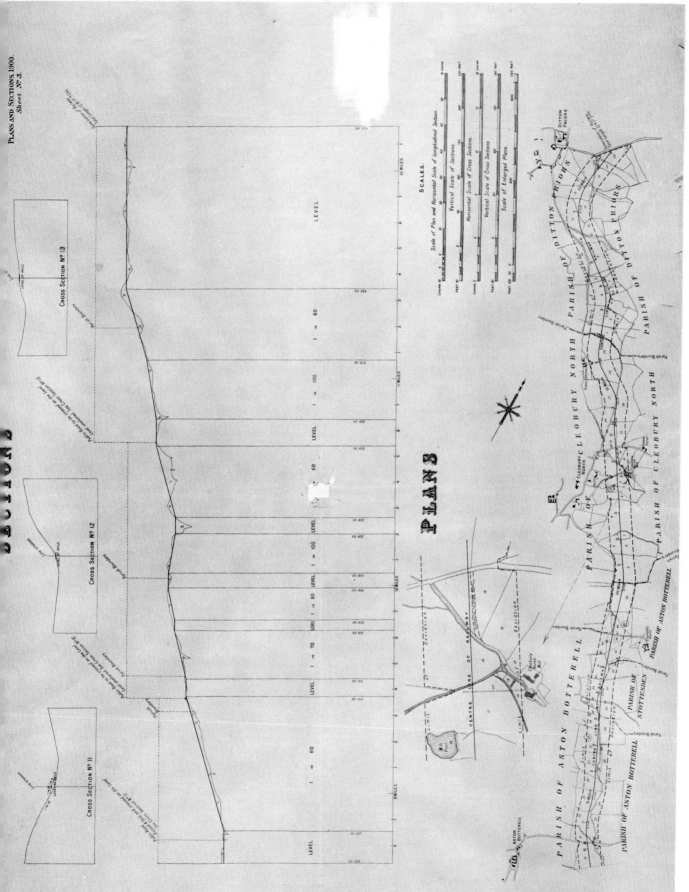

Plans and sections of the Cleobury Mortimer & Ditton Priors Light Railway.
Courtesy Stottesdon Parish Council

per day, excluding Sundays, Christmas Day and Good Friday. As an alternative to this they would take 60% of gross receipts plus an indemnity not exceeding £2,000 per year to be concluded when the line had reached the amount of working expenses at 2/- per mile for three consecutive years. The GWR stipulated that some indemnity be provided to their satisfaction, either by a private person or a bank and on no account from a company or limited company. Money was not readily available at this time and an appeal was made by the Directors to Lord Boyne to give further financial backing in order to meet the GWR's requirements. Hearing that this was not possible, the Board of Directors of the CM & DP Lt Rly felt that it was useless for them to continue in office as they had only accepted seats on the Board on the assurance of Lord Boyne's financial assistance and passed a resolution to this effect at a meeting on 25th November, 1901.

Matters dragged on into 1902 when J.T. Firbank & Co's tender of £100,000 to construct the line seemed, for a while, a likely possibility but foundered over financial problems.

1903 came and still no start on construction. Two tenders were received early in the year, one from Kerr Stuart & Co Ltd and one from Messrs Jackson & Co but neither bore fruit.

By 1904 the Board of Directors had seen nothing in return for their endeavours and the resignations of the Chairman, Sir Alexander Wilson, Kt and director Mr R.A. Klaglake were accepted in March 1904. Sir James de Houghton Bt and Mr G. Glasse-Hooper were elected in their place but did not remain long and resigned their seats in 1905 with still no start on construction work.

In the first month of 1906 a local contractor, Mr George Law of Kidderminster, put in a tender to construct and equip the line within 12 months for £86,500, £48,000 in cash and £38,500 in shares. The financial situation had eased somewhat by this time and there was a feeling that the construction would start at last. At the first Board meeting of the year in March, Mr Law's tender was given consideration. After some discussion his tender was agreed on, subject to conditions on both sides. For the Company, Mr Law would have to accept a contract drawn up by them and also Mr Law should have the quarry operational before the opening of the line, subject to the lease being given by Lord Boyne. For Mr Law, it was requested that he nominate his own engineer. This was accepted and Mr William T. Foxlee of Victoria Street, London was appointed at the next meeting even though the contract had not been signed. Mr Foxlee was no stranger to the Board, having been engaged on various tasks whilst Mr Calthrop was busy elsewhere. Mr Foxlee was given £500 on account for work done and his salary was fixed at 5% of all money used in the construction excluding land purchase but plus travelling expenses. Mr Caryl Roberts dissented from the appointment and asked for his protest at the exclusion of Mr Calthrop to be minuted. A letter was then sent to Mr Calthrop expressing the Board's regret at their "inability to further avail themselves of his services as engineer" and there followed a minor wrangle over expenses and compensation due to Mr Calthrop which was eventually settled to the satisfaction of both

sides in the argument. At this time, two new directors were appointed. They were Hon. Eustace Hamilton-Russell and Mr Dido Marshall.

In the spring of 1906 an application to the Board of Trade had to be made for an extension of time to the Order, and this was duly granted for the next year. The question of locomotives was also brought up, Messrs Kerr, Stuart having submitted some prints of plans for the Board's inspection. Mr Law's contract was still being discussed at Board level in May, and, in particular, it was noted that Mr Law could not guarantee Abdon Stone Quarry being operational before the line opened. The patience of the parties willing to finance the line was coming to an end and in June Mr Law was urged by letter either to complete the contract or abandon it, and in any case he was to consider negotiations to be at an end if no satisfactory arrangements had been made by 30th June, 1906.

Some concern was also being expressed now by the Board of Trade at the length of negotiations and it is at this point that the firm of Bott and Stennett first come into the story, marking the start of the long association of Mr William Stennett with the Company. On the 28th June, 1906, a representative of Bott and Stennett attended a Board meeting, and explained the construction company's willingness to quickly construct the line, form a company to work the Abdon Clee quarry and also to subscribe capital for such a company.

At this point it was voiced as a proposal, but as soon as Mr Law's contract fell through Bott and Stennett took over. In August 1906 Mr Stennett was appointed a director of the railway during its construction, at £100 per annum. It is interesting to note that the very next meeting of the Board, Mr Stennett stated that he could not guarantee the opening of the Abdon Clee quarry before the railway was finished, but this time the directors waived the point and the contract went ahead, signed in September 1906.

Mr Foxlee was still Engineer, and in the wake of the upsurge of activity asked the Board to allow him to set out the line, and to make new plans and sections.

One major change from Mr Calthrop's plan was in the siting of the junction with the Great Western Railway at Cleobury Mortimer. Here a much more compact arrangement of track, especially favourable to passengers transferring to and from Kidderminster or Tenbury trains, was agreed in November 1906. The altered site meant the CM & DP platform was now adjoining the GWR's with access to the booking hall. Apart from this, small changes in centre line did occur in places but the basic route remained unaltered.

This time a start was made, and by January 1907, Mr Foxlee was able to invite the contractors to begin work on any portion where the land had been acquired, and at the same meeting on 23rd January it was decided to cut the first sod but to do so without any of the traditional ceremony associated with the start of a railway's construction. So seven years after the Order was applied for, the Cleobury Mortimer and Ditton Priors Light Railway began to look a reality.

CHAPTER THREE

The Construction

ON the 25th January 1907 the contractors, Bott and Stennett, had possession of the land belonging to the Blount trustees from Cleobury Mortimer Junction to Wyre Crossing just over 1½ miles up the line.

It is possible to follow the progress of the construction from the monthly reports submitted by Engineer Foxlee to the CM & DP Lt Rly Secretary of the time, Mr Arthur Phillips. By February 1907, three cuttings beyond Cleobury Mortimer station had been started, and the building of the bridge 18 chains from Cleobury Mortimer station had begun together with the diversion of the small brook and the construction of a new culvert. By the middle of the year three of the sixteen cuttings between Cleobury Mortimer and Detton Ford (4 miles 4 chains) were finished and ten others were in hand. The Wilson steam navvy, seen in the photographs on pages 11 and 18, was operating at the south end of the earthworks making a long cutting through which the line rose steeply at 1:60 to Wyre Crossing. At this time too the northern section of the line was being tackled. Here was the largest tract of land purchased from one owner, 5 miles from Stottesdon to Ditton Priors, all belonging to Lord Boyne. It was in June 1907 that the line was joined permanently to the Great Western Railway when on 7th June, 1907, the contractor's temporary road was connected up with a junction at the Bewdley end of Cleobury Mortimer station.

By the July report the Steam navvy had reached the upper portion of the first major cutting, fencing was completed as far as Prescott (5 miles 4 furlongs), the major road bridge building was proceeding and work on the last two miles into Ditton Priors was continuing. The improved summer weather helped to keep progress brisk after a very wet May. Gates and fences enclosed the railway's property all the way towards the northern end, but even at this time the contractors still required possession of the land belonging to the Rev. T. Crump, Factory Cottages,

A comparison of Cleobury town station.
Above Excavating Cleobury Town yard in the Spring of 1907. Note the contractors' engine shed, Eveson private owner's wagon and wooden water tank. The railway company's offices are seen above the yard alongside the Bridgnorth Road.

W. Atkinson

Left The same scene around the time of the Grouping, with original wooden shed in the background. 0-6-0ST *Cleobury* leaves for Ditton Priors with four ex North London Railway coaches.

L&GRP

Excavating the rock cutting at 3m 15c, north of Chilton, showing Abdon Clee Stone Quarry Co. wagons. On the right can be seen Hunslet 0-6-0ST No. 761 *Uxbridge*.

W. Atkinson

Stottesdon, Mr John Sparrow's land at Prescott, and that of the Crumpton estate near Day House. Letters were received from "The Congress of Archaeological Societies" who expressed concern that the remains of early Neolithic, Bronze Age and Roman Camps on Abdon were in hourly danger of removal in the process of quarrying stone for railway ballast. They suggested a suspension of activities whilst the site was excavated but a further year's extension from the Board of Trade with an expiry date of 23rd May, 1908 had become necessary and the Railway were not prepared to accommodate the request.

Such was the ambitious enthusiasm amongst the general public now that additional money had been attracted, in particular a large loan from the Excess Insurance Company of London. The Lilleshall Company near Oakengates, Salop had applied for a coal wharf at Ditton Priors and at the annual Ditton Priors St Luke's Fair livestock auction in November 1907, opinion was voiced that a new auction yard would be opened as soon as the railway was completed and that there was likely to follow an increase over the four annual livestock auctions held there at the time.

Some time previously the Company had to reply to criticism from the Childe's estate at Kinlet for having delayed start to a coal mining project due to start in association with the new railway but now the opportunity arose to extend the rail link with the western edge of the Wyre Forest Coalfield.

In July 1907, at Bewdley, an inquiry was held into the proposed Kinlet Light Railway. Colonel Boughey and Mr A. Stewart, Light Railway Commissioners were there to decide the expediency of granting an application by Messrs Alfred Gibbs and Spencer Whatley for an Order for the construction of a Light Railway from Stottesdon through Kinlet to Billingsley. A very large attendance heard Mr Mayer propose the railway on behalf of the promoters. The line would pass chiefly through the land of Lord Barnard, Colonel Fisher Childe and the Crumpton trustees, all of whom supported the application to which there was no opposition.

The rich seams of coal, fire clay and brick earth beneath the

area were pointed out and the lack of suitable transport for local farmers to markets was also brought to the notice of the Commissioners. The directors of the CM & DP Lt Rly, it was mentioned, welcomed the application. The cost of the railway was estimated at £25,000 and the returns, it was thought would enable a dividend of 5% or more to be paid. The length of the railway would be 5½ miles and stations and halts were to be provided. Mr Foxlee, Engineer to the scheme, explained the wealth of the Billingsley Colliery to the Commissioners and added that timber traffic would also be forthcoming, as well as coal, off the Kinlet estate. There would be no difficulty raising the capital for the scheme, he concluded. Mr Gibbs of Billingsley Colliery gave his evidence as to the need for the railway as did Colonel Fisher Childe, his agent Mr Smith and agents of the Barnard and Crumpton estates. After several other local residents had added their weight, Colonel Boughey said he was satisfied as to the desirability of the railway and that it should be worked with the CM & DP Lt Railway.

With a year's work done, in the first month of 1908 the Wilson Steam Navvy was cutting out the site of Cleobury Town Yard, and can be seen doing this in the contractor's photographs. The spoil was moved back to fill the bank at the Cleobury Junction station with the wagons being hauled to the station by one of Bott and Stennett's locomotives.

The news of the death of the 8th Viscount Boyne on 30th December, 1907 aged 76, reached the Board of Directors just as the final sections of the line were being laid in place. He had watched, with great interest, the railway he promoted constructed across his estate but sadly did not live long enough to see the first official service in operation.

It is of interest to read here, extracts from a diary kept during the months of construction, by the Consultant Engineer to Bott and Stennett, Mr Walter Atkinson.

Actual work on our contract commenced in the February directly after taking up residence at Cleobury Mortimer. My staff included 'Busy' Dave Seamons (his place being taken later by Alf Russell), Harry Barlow (Foreman Mason), Slen Coe (Foreman Carpenter),

Harry Short (Foreman fitter), 'Big' Bill Overman (Foreman Platelayer), P.A. Wright (Cashier), Billy Hicks and Pickard (Timekeepers), George Laws (Horsekeeper), 'Gunner' Jim Neate, Jack Oliver, 'Gloucester' Roach, 'Warwick' Tom, 'Sleepy' Dick, Tom Cox and two or three other gangers.

Jack Oxlee (Chainman) was later put in charge of the gang. At the later period I had Herbert Wilson, son of John Wilson, Chief Engineer of the Great Eastern Railway, and a young man named Herriot as Assistant Engineers. For most part this was a very capable and efficient staff several of them having been associated with me on previous contracts. Mr William Foxlee of Westminster was the Consulting Engineer, and Mr Farrant was his Resident Engineer at the site. We established our offices and yard at the site of the new Cleobury Town Station on the main Bridgnorth road about a mile out of Cleobury Mortimer. We built two navvies huts at the Ditton Priors end and otherwise there was sufficient housing and lodging accommodation for our staff and men available in the district.

I had a horse and trap to take me to the various points along the works. In this connection, I purchased a first class iron-grey mare from Mr Bryan, Northwood Farm, Baveney Wood for the sum of 30 guineas which gave me excellent service right through the contract. She could take me from Ditton Priors to Cleobury Mortimer a distance of 11 miles in 1¼ hours. Also from Cleobury Mortimer to Kidderminster, a very hilly and heavy road of the same distance, in the same time.

I arranged with Dr Crow, "The Longlands", Cleobury Mortimer, and the genial Dr G.W. Cecil Hodges, Cleobury North to be our work's Doctors. I was to be very closely associated with the latter over the following years, and we became very friendly. I also met Mr Woodward and Mr Damon, GWR Engineers, at Cleobury Mortimer Station and made arrangements for the permanent junction connections to be installed. Generally speaking, the work on the contract presented no special engineering difficulties. The heaviest part of the work was concentrated in the first five miles from the Junction with the Great Western Railway at Cleobury Mortimer

station. On this portion we had a fair amount of heavy excavation in cuttings and several fair size embankments up to forty feet high. We employed a Wilson 12 ton crane type steam navvy to excavate the largest cuttings along the length. The material for the most was clay but we had to deal with the veins of rock in some of the cuttings. Where this rock was encountered we jumped holes down into it from the top ahead of the steam navvy, and blasted it with charges of "Chedite" supplied by Curtis and Harvey using an electric firing battery. We also met with some conglomerate rock in a cutting on the Nethercott Farm ground about three miles along the route. There were seven bridges, a two span covered way over Birmingham Water Mains and several fairly large culverts. All the bridges were designed on the contract and were of the arched type excepting one. They had abutments and wings built from the first class local Oreton limestone masonry. The arches, in all cases being in brickwork faced with Staffordshire brindled bricks. We used a very good brick for the backing work from the Hartlebury brickworks. Our largest bridge was one of two spans over the River Rea near Detton Ford about four miles along the route. This bridge contains first class examples of typical fitted snecked masonry. On this contract we utilised for the first time reinforced concrete pipes up to 3' 6" diameter for some of the culverts. These were very carefully handled and fixed. They were bedded on and flaunched with concrete and certainly made an economical and satisfactory culvert.

One of the problems we had to face was a small brook passing under the railway near the Great Western station and we installed a 2" Tangye steam force pump at this point.

The water was pumped a distance of nearly two miles into two supply tanks and gravitated through pipes from these to where it was required. We also installed a similar supply with a Worthington pump from a good spring on Miss Haywood's farm at Neen Savage. I well remember the arrangements made with Miss Haywood in connection with this. Alf Russell, our General Foreman, and I called to see her to obtain permission to install the pump and lay the necessary pipes across one of her meadows. After I explained our

Excavating the cutting at 1m 25c near Mawley Town. Some of the crew are: (second left) Turpin Laws, (fourth left) Frank Spinnager, (sixth left) Tom Spinnager, (fourth right) Tom Dallaway — "wagon spragger", (third right) Ted Dallaway, and Jim Spinnager in the cab of the steam navvy. Note the wooden "sprag" braking the front wheel of the wagon.

W. Atkinson

Photograph, elevation and plan of the Duddlewick overbridge as built in 1907.
Photograph W. Atkinson
Plan courtesy C. Eyre

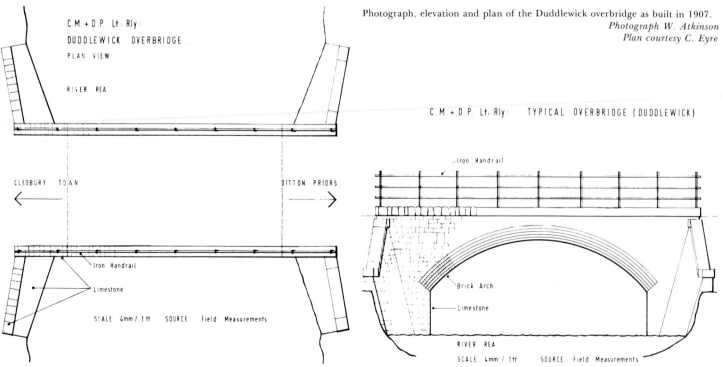

C.M.+D.P. Lt. Rly:
DUDDLEWICK OVERBRIDGE.
PLAN VIEW

RIVER REA

CLEOBURY TOWN   DITTON PRIORS

Iron Handrail

Limestone

SCALE 4mm / 1ft   SOURCE Field Measurements

C.M. + D.P. Lt. Rly: TYPICAL OVERBRIDGE (DUDDLEWICK)

Iron Handrail

Brick Arch

Limestone

RIVER REA

SCALE 4mm / 1ft.   SOURCE Field Measurements

Three of the locomotives used during the construction of the line. *Top* Manning, Wardle 0-6-0ST class "K" No. 626 *Trent*, later sold to the Abdon Clee Stone Quarry Company. *Centre* Hunslet 0-4-0ST No. 525 *Canada*. *Bottom* Hudswell, Clarke 0-6-0ST No. 621 *Lily*, sold at Cleobury Mortimer in 1911.

W. Atkinson

requirements, she considered the request and explained that she had no objection to letting us have the water on the understanding that we paid her the sum of £2 for the facility. I turned round to Alf and asked if he thought the amount was reasonable. He, very tactfully, replied that in his opinion it was quite a fair offer. We paid over the money and Miss Haywood produced a jug of cider to properly seal the bargain. Some time after the transaction, I met Miss Haywood's brother John. He referred to this water supply and said that if he had been consulted he would have advised his sister not to let us have the water under the sum of £10. I could have told him that, if necessary, we should have been prepared to pay £50 for the facility. However I have no qualms of conscience over this matter. The facts were that the water we pumped would otherwise have run to waste, and as our pipes were simply laid on the grass there was no damage to the field.

The following are two water supply episodes which occurred on this contract: — soon after commencing work, I applied to Fred. W. Macauley, Chief Engineer of the Birmingham Waterworks, for a temporary connection to one of their 3' 6" diameter mains which crossed the line of our railway near Cleobury Town Station. In due course he replied regretting that they could not see their way to giving us temporary service, it being their settled policy not to allow their mains to be tapped for this purpose. Some weeks after our application had been turned down a serious burst occurred in one of the mains on the top of a steep slope about two miles from our railway. This burst washed out a large crater, the debris from this being swept down the slope. After the pipeline had been repaired steps had to be taken to fill up the crater. In connection with this, Mr Warwick, the Assistant Waterwork's Engineer, and the length's walksman, appropriately named Walker, came to see me to enquire if we would loan them some of our 2ft gauge 'Decauville' railway track and wagons to help them out of their difficulty. I told them we should be pleased to oblige, and placed the required materials at their disposal. When the question was raised to what recompense they should pay us for loan of the tracks and wagons, I informed Mr Warwick that we did not want or expect any cash repayment but if they would reconsider our application for a temporary connection it would be of material assistance in the supply of water to our steam navvy and locomotive which would shortly be at work at Cleobury Town Station site.

The old adage 'one good turn deserves another' bore fruit in the case and we got our much needed connection. Subsequently this was a definite asset to the railway company as our original temporary service became permanent and supplied an umbrella tank which the Company erected at Cleobury Town station to water their locomotives.

Soon after commencing the excavation of a longish shallow cutting about 7½ miles up the line, we came up with a 2" cast iron waterpipe which passed right along the cutting at a depth of 2' 6" below the surface. This particular land was part of Viscount Boyne's large Burwarton estate, so I called his agent, Mr Jack Pierce, to make enquiries about this mysterious pipe. He was able to inform me that it was a water supply from a spring in a field near Aston Botterell to two farms at Duddlewick. This pipe was about two miles long and had been installed many years before when the Duke of Cleveland owned the estate. The spring was situated in an arable field and the estate office could give me no definite information as to the actual location. I got in touch with the oldest inhabitant at Aston Botterell and he was able to give the approximate position as far as he could remember. We put one or two of our men to probe the ground with heavy crowbars, and, after spending most of the day on this work, eventually located the spring. We found a proper little chamber had been built at the inlet of the pipe, and this was covered with a slab, the whole being buried about a foot below the surface, presumably so as not to interfere with ploughing operations. Subsequently, we put the necessary pipe diversion clear of our cutting. Incidentally, the discovery of this pipe enabled us to install two or three automatic water tanks to supply certain fields which had been cut off from the river by the Railway.

The access to the site where our steam navvy was to commence operation was difficult so we decided to build her in the GWR goods yard at Cleobury Mortimer station utilising the Railway Company's Crane for the erection and then travel her to the required site under her own steam. To do this we had to travel the main Kidderminster road for a short distance which involved passing under the railway bridge. I had previously written to Mr Lewis Jones asking him to send me the overall height of the navvy minus the detachable chimney. Working on the measurements he gave me, I found that these would be just sufficient clearance for the machine to pass under the bridge. Directly the navvy was erected in the goods yard, I took a measurement to check the height and was surprised to find it was something like a foot more that was given by Mr Jones. This unfortunate error of course, placed us in a bit of a quandary, and was one of those unexpected problems that frequently arise on public works.

'Busy' Dave Seamons had one of his brainwaves and suggested that the best way out of the difficulty would be to lower the highway to give us the necessary headroom. After consideration, we decided that this method would be best so I went off post-haste to Shrewsbury to see Mr Davies, the County Surveyor and Engineer. After listening to my tale of woe, he kindly consented to our proposal to lower the road on the understanding that we carried out the work on a Sunday, and reinstated the road in a satisfactory and proper manner. We successfully accomplished our task and the steam navvy was travelled to the required site without undue incident.

The various farmers along the route were without exception extremely helpful. It was my invariable practice to offer them any occasional haulage or horse hire work which had to be done on their particular farms, and this was of considerable assistance to us in the early stages on the contract when fencing and other materials had to be carried across the fields some distance from the public roads. I well remember walking out to Nethercott Farm on a Sunday morning with our Foreman Carpenter Slen Coe to see a tenant, Mrs Corbett, about some cartage across her land. She invited us to partake of some prime perry which, of course, was very acceptable after our three miles walk. Not being acclimatised to this potent beverage, I asked to be excused when Mrs Corbett asked us to have another helping. Although I warned him of the possible consequences, Slen Coe could not resist the temptation and quaffed a further pint. As we were passing along the lane about halfway on our return walk to Cleobury Mortimer, Slen turned to me and remarked that he wished that he had taken my advice and not indulged in the extra pint of perry. He thereupon made a quick bolt through the nearest gap in the hedge. All the farmers in the district kept hogsheads of cider and perry, and it was their usual custom to invite callers to partake of this wholesome refreshment. Mr & Mrs Bray at the Day House half way along the railway always gave me a kindly welcome. I generally called there once a week. It was my "Half Way House".

There was a delay of nine months in obtaining possession of a field of Glebe land at Cleobury North. This was the property of Ecclesiastical Commissioners. I thought it was typical of the tardiness and difficulty in acquiring land belonging to the Church. To avoid delay to the progress of our work, I called on the vicar, the Reverend Bush, and he kindly gave us permission, without prejudice, to put in a temporary overland railway across the field until the transfer of the required land had been formally completed.

The main purpose of our new railway was to tap the undeveloped deposits of Clee Hill basalt rock situated at the crest of the Brown Clee Hill at Ditton Priors on Viscount Boyne's estate. He was, personally very interested in the project and I conducted him over our works on one or two occasions.

His son, The Hon. Eustace Hamilton-Russell, also took a keen interest in this scheme and paid us periodic visits. A new company, The Abdon Clee Stone Company Ltd had been formed to open up and develop a quarry at Ditton Priors. Both Mr Bott and Mr Stennett were directors and had financial interests in this new Company, also Mr Eustace Hamilton-Russell. This Clee basalt, locally called dhustone, was one of the finest road making stones in the country. Deposits of similar stone on the Titterstone Clee Hill had been quarried on a large scale for a considerable number of years with railway access via Ludlow. The market for the stone extended over many counties even to such a distant county as Hampshire. Some time before we had completed our railway, the Abdon Company commenced operations on the construction of their inclined railway and private sidings to link the quarry with our terminus at Ditton Priors. This involved some interesting engineering work including three bridges. The incline railway was constructed to handle main line wagons. For a distance of two thousand yards the steepest portion of the incline was operated by heavy wire cables controlled by a large 18' diameter winding drum at the top. The ends of the cable were attached to special brake wagons and as the full load of two or three wagons containing twenty or thirty tons ran down the incline by gravity, a set of empties was being pulled up. The two sets passing each other en route at a special passing loop in the centre of the incline. The speed of the wagons controlled by 6" band brakes on a winding drum. The gradient on one part of this incline was as steep as 1 in 4½. A six wheeled steam locomotive was employed to work the wagons over the lower portion of the incline, a distance of about ½ mile where the gradient did not exceed 1 in 20. The drum brake mechanism was designed and supplied by Messrs Howard, Engineers, Bedford. When the trial was made it was found that the brakes could not be properly applied so the wagons got out of control and several were badly damaged. After certain modifications had been made, the drum did its work in a satisfactory manner and subsequently dealt with many thousands of tons of material.

All the heavy crushing, screening and other plant to be installed in the quarry was taken up this incline. To the best of my recollection, the difference in level between the sidings at Ditton Priors station and the quarry floor was about 800'. I well remember a Mr Richards, quarry owner from Rowley Regis being very much impressed with the incline and his remark that it required both pluck and money to carry out such an undertaking. Just as work on the incline was approaching completion an unfortunate fatal accident occurred to one of our locomotive drivers named Ben Revell.

Turning, at this point, to a report in the *Bridgnorth Journal* we find that the inquest into Driver Revell's death was held at Oakwood Farm, Ditton Priors in May 1908. Jack Strong (driver), called as witness, said

On Sunday morning at about 8 am we started to go up the inclined railway with two trucks. The trucks were in front and there were two engines behind. Both engines were working. We started from the Oakwood bridge on the level. When we had gone about 100 yards to where the incline gets steeper we found that the engines could not push the tracks up. We came back to where we started and took off one truck and started with the other one which was full of ashes, I was driving the first engine and Revell the second. We got about ¼ mile up the incline and found we could get no further. The weight of the truck pushed both engines back and they both began to skid. We put on full steam forward and we put on the brakes. The wheels still skidded backwards. They went slow at first but gained speed down the incline and swayed a good deal. Both engines and truck left the rails after going about ¼ mile but both engines remained upright.

Mr Strong stated that they had been on similar trips up the incline before the accident. John Posterns, the pointsman, was on Revell's engine. He reported to the inquest how Mr Revell put on the brake and then full steam without being able to stop the slide. Mr Posterns continued "Revell was behind me with one foot on the edge of the footplate holding onto the brake. The engine shook very much and Revell said 'Hold tight, boy'. I saw his hand loose the brake but could not see any more for the steam". When the engine stopped it had derailed, Revell was missing from the cab and they found him in the four foot way quite dead, the other engine having passed over him. Mr Alfred Russell, Foreman on the day, was unable to explain why the engines could not push their load up the incline although the gradient at the point that they stopped was 1 in 13. The Coroner summed up the accident as having no clear cause and directed

the jury to conclude that it was an accidental death.
Mr Atkinson continues in his diary:

Ben was a highly respected driver with a long experience on public works and his death came as a shock to us all. It was my sad duty to break the news to his wife living at Lower Street, Cleobury Mortimer. She was suffering with heart trouble, so I took our work's Doctor with me in case of need. I never forgot the brave manner in which she faced this sudden tragic ordeal. This was the only fatal accident that occurred to any of our men on the contract.

My friend 'Busy' Dave Seamons who had been transferred sometime previously to another contract in North Wales came back to Ditton Priors to organise and superint the difficult task of getting the Quarry Company's heavy plant, which included a locomotive, conveyed up the incline. The work was accomplished in a safe and satisfactory manner, a definite tribute to this fine foreman's capabilities under extraordinary conditions.

Sometime after work on this railway commenced, the Clee Hill Company decided to develop a new quarry at the Magpie Quarry on the East side of Titterstone Clee and link this up with a cableway on our sidings at Detton Ford.

Mr Grover carried out the survey and superintendence of this interesting project. The cableway was 3¾ miles long with one angle station and was designed, supplied and erected by Messrs Hendersons the well known engineers of Aberdeen. The overhead cableway which was mounted on steel pylons conveyed tubs holding ten cwt of stone, the whole movement being automatic. It was a most economic and effective way of handling the material. On completion a test for capacity was made and it was found that the cableway would be able to deal with up to 60 tons per hour which was very much in excess with the output of the quarrying plant.

Before our railway was completed we carried out survey work and made a rough estimate for a branch line from our Stottesden Station to the Billingsley Colliery. At this time this pit had not rail access and depended entirely on land sale. My assistant, Herbert Wilson, carried out the survey work and I very well remember that his father, John Wilson, Chief Engineer of the Great Eastern Railway paid us a visit. At this time Herbert was engaged on plotting the gradients on the longitudinal sections. He was evidently most interested in his son's work and imparted some fatherly advice. This branch line scheme, however, did not materialise. Negotiations had been going on in another direction which resulted in the Powell Duffryn Company acquiring the Billingsley Colliery. They decided to get rail access to the GWR Severn Valley line by means of a connection at the existing Kinlet Colliery. It is of special interest to record that Messrs Caffin & Co. secured the contract for the construction of this Billingsley Railway. This was one of the first contracts to be carried out by this firm. Mr Herbert A. Caffin had previously severed his connections with Oliver and Sons, Railway Contractors. The job was commenced in 1908 at the time when work on our Ditton Priors Railway was well forward. I well remember one of our locomotive drivers, George Fullaway, a very good man, left us to go to work for Mr Caffin at Billingsley. Little did I realise, at the time, that I was to become associated with him over a long period of years.

The influx of railway navvies must have added considerably to the population of the quiet Rea valley. The photographs show clearly the large size of the labour force employed on such a contract. Railway navvies had a bad reputation for disorderly behaviour at this time, so it is not surprising to find some correspondence between the Chief Constable of Shropshire and Bott and Stennett concerning the appointment of a special constable at Cleobury Mortimer to supervise the gangs but in the event it was considered unnecessary. There was, however, a reference to the navvies at the Cleobury Mortimer Brewster Sessions of 8th February, 1908 under the chairmanship of Mr Henry C.V. Hunter.

Supt Perry reported an increase over the year in offences against the licensing laws proceeded with from 13 in 1906 to 28 persons in 1907. This increase he attributed mainly to the men employed on the construction of the CM & DP Lt Rly.

CHAPTER FOUR

Early Rolling Stock

IT had become clear, by March 1908, that the time had come to consider the rolling stock needed by the CM & DP Lt Rly, Mr Foxlee therefore took tenders from a roll call of locomotive manufacturers of the day. The following put in bids to supply locomotives to the CM & DP Lt Rly:— Andrew Barclay, Sons & Co Ltd, W.G. Bagnall Ltd, Beyer, Peacock and Co Ltd, Hunslet Engine Co Ltd, Kitson & Co Ltd, Manning, Wardle and Co Ltd, North British Locomotive Co Ltd, and Robert Stephenson and Co Ltd.

Up until this time the stock had, of course, been provided by the contractors, Bott and Stennett, who brought with them their own wagons (with a large "B and S" on their sides), with the addition of a large quantity of the Abdon Clee Stone Quarry Co wagons some of which can be seen in use in the photographs. Fortunately we have from the notes of Mr Walter Atkinson, Consultant Engineer, to Bott and Stennett, details of the locomotives employed on the CM & DP Lt Rly contract and photographs of five of them. Several of these locos had been employed previously on the Harrow and Uxbridge Railway "Bott and Stennett's most important contract", according to Mr Walter Atkinson. The contractor's locos were as follows:—

Wheel Arr.	Loco Name	Manufacturer	Makers No.	Year of Building
0-6-0ST	Lily	Hudswell, Clarke & Co Ltd	621	1902
0-4-0ST	Canada	Hunslet Engine Co Ltd	525	1890
0-6-0ST	Fleetwood	Hudswell, Clarke & Co Ltd	318	1888
0-6-0ST	Kingswood*	Manning, Wardle & Co Ltd	729	1880
0-6-0ST	Trent	Manning, Wardle & Co Ltd	626	1876
0-6-0ST	Uxbridge	Hunslet Engine Co Ltd	761	1902

* Previously known as *Record Reign* bought secondhand and sold to the Abdon Clee Quarry Co, as were *Trent* and *Fleetwood*.

There was a letter from Mr Foxlee to Secretary Mr Arthur Phillips, following a personal inspection of some Peckett locomotives at Neasden, in which Mr Foxlee expressed the view that "no doubt they will suit our requirements very well". He went on to detail the supply situation which was that Peckett's could supply one engine in six weeks and two in two months and added "Manning, Wardle make very good engines but their price is too high". However by April, Mr Foxlee had reconsidered this, in view of new plans to buy the necessary locomotives on hire purchase and suggested that an order should be placed through his agent Mr William Jones of Upper Thames Street, London for two tank locos with vacuum brakes from Manning, Wardle of Leeds. The cost was £1,970 each delivered to Cleobury Mortimer; or, spread over 5 years, twenty quarterly payments of £188 plus £370 per engine to be paid on delivery.

How much this easy payment scheme influenced the Board to decide upon the Manning, Wardle pair is unknown but it is also interesting to note, in passing, that Viscount Boyne's family had land in Yorkshire and had sold part of the estate which bordered the works of E.B. Wilson, and enabled the expansion of the firm that grew out of Wilson's of Leeds, to become the same Manning, Wardle and Company. However, the choice was made and the order placed in April 1908 with delivery dates promised June 17th and 30th of the same year. The makers numbers were 1734 and 1735, 1734 was named *Burwarton* after Lord Boyne's estate and 1735 was given the name *Cleobury*. They were 0-6-0ST with 3'6" diameter wheels and incorporating a number of typical Manning, Wardle features most notably the raised round topped firebox and the flat sided saddle tank above the running plate. Below the footplate the brake hangers were pivoted from the frame at their lower extremities instead of, more conventionally, from the top.

Livery was a medium green with black lining edged red and yellow. Frames were black with wheels, frames and cylinders picked out in yellow. The names were carried on brass plates with 3¾" letters standing out against a vermilion background.

The two locomotives were not quite identical, and it is possible to see in the photographs differences in the pipework and injectors on the left hand side of the locomotives. The tank filler caps were different as well, but the principal dimensions were standard and are as follows:—

Manning, Wardle 0-6-0ST No. 1734 *Burwarton* at Cleobury Town. Shunter Treacy on left, Driver Strong on right.

W. Atkinson

Gauge of railway	4 ft 8½ in
Diameter of coupled wheels	3 ft 6 in
Wheelbase	4 ft 10 in + 5 ft 8 in =10 ft 6 in
Empty weights	Ldg axle 10 t 6 cwt 2 q
Driving axle	13 t 4 cwt 2 q
Trailing axle	11 t 5 cwt 0 q
Total	37 t 16 cwt 0 q
Size of cylinders	Diameter 16 in Stroke 22 in
Boiler pressure	160 lb
Diameter of boiler barrel	4 ft 0 in
Length of boiler barrel	9 ft 2 in
Number of tubes	167
Diameter of tubes	1⅞ in o/d
Tube heating surface	773 sq ft
Firebox heating surface	83 sq ft
Total heating surface	855 sq ft
Grate area	14 sq ft
Tank capacity	890 gallons
Tractive effort	18,235 lb

The two engines were late being finished and did not leave Manning, Wardle's until August 13th and arrived at Cleobury to run trial trips on the 20th August. By this time of course several staff had been taken on and in the early photographs we see Driver Tom Dowding, who had driven Great Western Dean Singles on the London-Bristol route before coming to Cleobury Mortimer. Mr Dowding came to work on the CM & DP Lt Rly as a result of a doctor's advice to his sick wife to get away from London air and into the country. Mr Dowding had been born at Ross in Herefordshire and his wife came originally from Cheshire so lodging at Wakemans, The Wells, Cleobury Mortimer were most convenient until the tenancy of "Whitegates" in Cleobury Mortimer became vacant for Mr Dowding.

The 3'6" wheels of Nos. 1734 and 1735 were in marked contrast to the size of the huge drivers on the GWR singles and Mr Dowding's son, Geoffrey, can recall his father's opinion that the wheels of the Manning, Wardles were too small to give sufficient power with a full load of stone wagons.

By the time the locos had arrived for their trial trips, other appointments had been made, notably Mr Ernest Morris who had become Manager in May 1908, having previously had very good experience as a station master and later a goods canvasser with the Metropolitan Railway.

The contractors by now had sold their locos *Trent*, *Fleetwood* and *Kingswood* to the Abdon Clee Stone Quarry Co Ltd and as the Manning, Wardles were late being delivered, the first goods service on the CM & DP was operated by these contractors locos for a fee of 50% of the gross receipts.

Such good progress on construction had been possible in the year 1908 that Mr Morris was able to commence his goods service on 19th July, and run a daily goods train thereafter, but the Board of Trade had not approved the line for passenger services at this time. When Nos. 1734 and 1735 arrived in August, there was quite a considerable correspondence between Mr Morris and Manning, Wardle & Co over the tendency of the two locomotives to overheat. It was stated by Mr Morris that the brasses in the axleboxes of both engines had no channel-way, and it was eventually proposed to lift *Cleobury* in the presence of representatives of Manning, Wardle and to confirm this fact to them. Manning, Wardle & Co then wrote to Mr Morris stating

quite clearly that the engines had left their works with correctly cut channel-ways and suggesting poor lubrication at Cleobury Town shed was the likely cause of the trouble. At the lifting of *Cleobury*, Manning, Wardle's representative found what he described as "serious neglect". The horn cheeks were all more or less scored, one being $^1/_{16}$ inch deep. The axlebox brasses were also all scored and one had been so badly neglected that the brass had stuck to the axle and had to be knocked off with a heavy hammer whilst in three of the brasses the grease grooves were worn away. Manning, Wardle therefore felt entitled to their initial payment which had been held back and from this time on, the locomotives ran satisfactorily and did not overheat.

Passenger rolling stock was also bought through Mr Jones of Upper Thames Street, London in readiness for the anticipated opening of the passenger service in November 1908. Mr Foxlee had been to inspect the alterations being made to four North London coaches at Bow Works, London and had expressed his satisfaction with the progress on them. The purchase consisted of four wheeled stock fitted with vacuum brakes, and all four were 28ft x 8ft x 6ft 8ins dimensions on a 15ft wheelbase. The North London duplicate numbers of 1033, 1034, 1041 and 1043 were altered to the CM & DP Lt Railway number 1, 2, 3 and 4. Numbers 1 and 3 were of three third class compartments and a luggage compartment whereas number 2 and 4 had four third class compartments and one first fitted into each at Mr Foxlee's instructions. They kept their old livery of varnished teak, black underframe and a grey roof. Lettering colour is unknown but most likely to be shaded gold. Numbers 2 and 4 had their first class entrance in the middle of the coach and had an extra set of footsteps below this door, in contrast to the steps at either end only on numbers 1 and 3, the original footboards having been removed from all four coaches. At Bow Works, bars were taken off the windows and the buffers changed to suit the CM & DP Lt Rly but the safety chains on the buffer beam left on. The major change made for the new owners can be seen on page 317 of the April, 1909 *Railway Magazine*. This shows the position of a communication door built into one end of each of the coaches allowing the guard to transfer from one vehicle to another across an open platform. The object of this construction was to allow the guard to collect fares from all travellers as the train moved along its journey. The class of the compartment was denoted in words below each droplight and again with a numeral on a raised panel on each door. The cost of these secondhand coaches was £65 each with £25 allowed for alterations, the whole purchase being spread over seven years. The lighting was by oil and in a letter from Mr Morris dated September 1909 he complained about a poor sample of oil which was giving him problems keeping the lamps burning on the winter evening journeys. Apart from this the four coaches gave good and continuous service as soon as the passenger service began.

The other item of rolling stock needed by the new railway was open goods wagons to haul the dhustone away onto the rest of Britain's railway system. The Abdon Clee Stone Quarry Company had bought some wagons from the British Wagon Company of Rotherham (taken over in 1967 by United Dominions Trust Ltd). These wagons were four plank 10 ton vehicles and lettered in three known styles:-

The first style was "Abdon Clee Stone Quarry" on the top plank with "Company Ltd" and the wagon number in smaller lettering on the second plank. No shading is apparent on this lettering. On later photographs the wagon number can be seen in a different position on the left hand of the second plank down and on this version the lettering appears shaded. Another

Above Train in Ditton Priors station at the time of the opening, showing locomotive taking water from wooden tank. The original levers on the turnout were later changed.

R.C. Riley Collection

Right 0-6-0ST *Burwarton* at Cleobury Town with ex North London Railway coach.

R.C. Riley Collection, per S. Morris

Left 0-6-0ST *Cleobury* with brake van No. 2 in second livery at Ditton Priors. From left to right: Driver Tom Dowding, Fireman Jim Howe, Guard Ted Teague. Note variations on injectors and tank filler cap from *Burwarton* on page 24.

Real Photographs

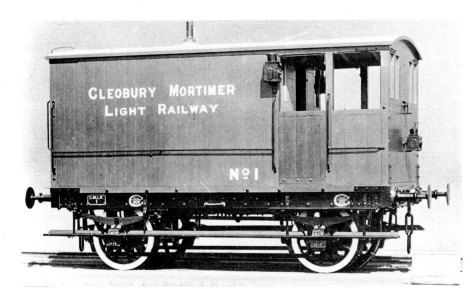

A works photograph of goods brake van No. 1 in original livery.

Courtesy HMRS

lettering style has "Abdon Clee Stone Quarry Co" on the top plank and "Ditton Priors" covering the next two planks down and arranged with one word either side of the door. It is suggested that these wagons had a red oxide body colour at first but from photographs and local evidence some, at least, appear a shade of grey with black ironwork on the body and underframe. The wagons were numbered on the ends as well as the sides.

Here should be mentioned two other sets of Private Owner wagons directly associated with the line from the very start of goods traffic and more will be said later about their links with the CM & DP Lt Rly. The wagons were "Clee Hill Granite Company", moving to and from Detton Ford sidings and "Burwarton Coal and Trading Company, Cleobury Mortimer" based at Cleobury Town and Ditton Priors. CM & DP Lt Rly decided to have their own open wagons from the British Wagon Company and ordered ten in March 1908 on hire purchase terms of £64.10s (£64.50p) over seven years including painting and repair costs. These wagons were numbered 1 to 10 and were 9ft wheelbase 10 ton capacity wagons very similar if not the same, as the 10 ton capacity Abdon Clee Quarry Company wagons. Later an additional ten wagons ordered in 1912, were supplied by the British Wagon Company as "converted" wagons of 8ft wheelbase and 8 ton capacity. This tonnage was queried at the time by the CM & DP manager when he quoted the dimensions (14'6" x 7' x 2'4") as being the same as the original

ten which had 2 tons higher capacity. It was one of the second batch that Mr K.A. Werrett recorded at Woodchester (M.R.) goods yard in 1917. Also, in 1912, a request was made to letter the wagons in the style "Cleobury Mortimer Light Railway Company" which may have been a reversion to an earlier form of Company inscription seen on the photographs of the brake vans. These two sturdy vans were built to order at the Gloucester Carriage and Wagon Co Ltd in 1908 for a cost of £211 each. They were 10ft wheelbase vehicles and with a tare weight of 19½ tons were able to control the heaviest mineral trains. They were light grey in colour, like the open wagons, and at first were lettered "Cleobury Mortimer Light Railway" but later the Ditton Priors connection was included in the labelling and they became "C.M. and D.P. Lt Rly" nos 1 and 2, thereby duplicating the numbers of two open wagons.

The railway was now set up with the basic requirements for its own immediate needs as far as rolling stock was concerned. To the above descriptions should be added a 5 ton travelling crane which the Light Railway owned which, no doubt, assisted with timber haulage from Lord Boyne's estate but no provision was made for rolling stock to convey the other category of goods that the railway set out to gain, namely the movement of perishable farm produce and livestock to and from markets.

Everything was now ready for the first passengers once the final inspection of the line had been completed.

CM & DP wagon No. 10 forming part of a stone train at Shipton (GWR).

Packer Studios

Cleobury Mortimer (GWR) in Summer 1907. The CM & DP sidings with original style stop block can be seen on the left. The signal box was later enlarged by the GWR.

W. Atkinson

CHAPTER FIVE

The Line in 1908

FOLLOWING the satisfactory opening of the freight service on 19th July, 1908, preparations were put in hand towards getting the line into good condition ready for inspection by the Board of Trade. Mr Foxlee, no doubt anticipating that the inspector would be favourable towards the CM & DP Lt Rly, wrote to the Board of Directors expressing his hope that the passenger service would commence on 16th November, 1908 after the inspector's visit, which he had confirmed as the 13th November, 1908.

The Inspecting officer of the CM & DP Lt Rly was Lieutenant-Colonel H.A. Yorke, Assistant Secretary to the railway department of the Board of Trade who was accompanied on the special train that day by the Directors, the Engineer and other interested parties.

The Inspecting officer's train, on leaving Cleobury Mortimer Junction (GWR) passed over the Bewdley-Cleobury Mortimer road close by the Blount Arms Hotel and briefly touched the westernmost point of the extensive Wyre Forest at Coachroad Coppice.

The engine soon had to work hard as the line sharply turned westward and the gradient stiffened to 1 in 60. A brief glimpse of Weston Farm on the left, and after passing through several cuttings the train reached the summit of the rise to Mawley Town road crossing (or Wyre Common crossing) the first of many ungated crossings (1m 38½ ch from Cleobury Junction).

From this crossing the fireman could relax as the train gently dropped down before halting at the gates across the Bridgnorth road. The gates were swung open by the fireman and the train moved slowly forward, drawing to a halt at Cleobury Town, the first station on the line, and also the Railway's headquarters (1m 78½ ch from Cleobury Junction). The Town station was, in fact, a great deal nearer to the centre of Cleobury Mortimer than the GWR station at the Junction, and later could easily be reached on foot from Cleobury Mortimer by a short walk via the Paper Mill bridge over the nearby river Rea.

Bridge over Cleobury Mortimer Road, 1908. The bridge in the background carried the GWR Tenbury line. Just visible beyond that is the Blount Arms with a brewer's dray delivering.

W. Atkinson

Burwarton breasts the summit of the 1 in 60 gradient with a freight train near Wyre Common Crossing.   *R.C. Riley Collection*

The wooden railway offices at this time stood alongside the Bridgnorth road overlooking the station site on the edge of a small coppice and were originally the temporary offices of the contractors, now on hire from them, as was also a one road wooden engine shed which had formerly housed the contractor's locos.

The wooden station building was identical to others constructed at Stottesdon, Burwarton and Ditton Priors and consisted of a porters room, waiting room, but differed in that it was situated not on the platform, but a few yards from it. The reason for this is not clear. The platform was similar to the others along the line, being at this time 1ft high with a surface of crushed stone, whilst the wooden platform edges were painted white. Name boards, lamps and white fences added a final touch to give a thoroughly neat and tidy appearance.

The station yard had a passing loop and siding to the engine shed plus a cattle dock (for the intended livestock traffic) near which was a wagon loading gauge. At the Ditton Priors end of the station platform was a small timber water tank for the locomotives, the only one between here and the terminus.

The area of land excavated by the railway at Cleobury Town was far in excess of its needs, but was ideal for one use to which it was put. For some years the Burwarton Coal and Trading Company occupied a site in the yard and quoting from the diary of Mr Atkinson we can record something of this Company's beginning:

. . . realizing that the new railway to Ditton Priors would open up new territory for trade, we formed the "Burwarton Coal and Trading Company" to develop this trade and commercial business in August 1908. The original founders and partners in the company were Dr G.W. Cecil Hodges, Cleobury North; Mr William Williamson, The Bold, Burwarton, J.T. Shingler, Cleobury North; and myself. The Doctor was chairman and I was appointed manager at Cleobury Mortimer. The main purpose was to trade in coal, coke, cement and lime and all classes of building material including timber and joinery work. Depots were established at Cleobury Town and Ditton Priors stations. Messrs Harry Southern and Sons who had a haulage business at Ditton Priors became our agents in that developing district. The public were quick to appreciate the facilities we were able to give and so the company was

Above Cleobury Town in 1908, showing one of the first goods trains before the contractors had removed their track. Note that the station shelter is separate from the platform.

T. Davies Collection

Below The Clee Hill Granite Company's aerial ropeway terminus at Detton Ford in 1927. Seen in this view are Archie Southern (holding the shunting horse), Simon Evans (left centre) and Edwin Martin (right centre).

Courtesy E. Wall

soon doing a rapidly expanding business. I always consider the services rendered by this company were an undoubted boon to the scattered residents of this out of the way countryside.

After taking on water the train was off again dropping downgrade from the level of the Town station across the Six Ashes-Neen Savage road (Neen Lane crossing) towards Chilton siding (2m 58½ ch). Here was a small platform and siding put in at the request of Mr Michael Tomkinson and was to be a bone of contention for some years. Originally it was to be called Neen Savage. From here the line undulated till Detton Ford (originally to be called Detton Mill), 4m 26ch was reached. At this point the party witnessed work being carried out to link the railway with the quarries on the Eastern side of the Titterstone Clee, some 4 miles away. Stone from these quarries was of a similar nature to the Abdon stone, and there had been a scheme to link the Magpie Quarry, by rail over Catherton Common to Detton Ford but it is not surprising that it was soon shelved considering the marshy nature of the ground it would have had to traverse. However the enterprising Captain Roberts, owner of Clee Hill Granite Company, had other ideas. He decided on an aerial ropeway, very much the vogue at that time, to transport the stone down to Detton Ford sidings. Agreement had already been reached in March 1908 with the Lt. Railway, for a siding connection with a discharge terminal. A payment of £685-13-0 (£685.65p) for the alterations received by the Light Railway Board in October concluded the agreement, enabling the work to be carried out.

The ropeway at the time of inspection was not operational but the 56 trestles carrying the 7 miles of continuous steel rope, supplied by a local firm, Edges of Shifnal, were already standing out gaunt against the wintry Titterstone Clee skyline. Climbing away from Detton the train immediately crossed the River Rea on a 30ft span bridge partly constructed of fine limestone from a local quarry at nearby Oreton, then owned by Mr Tom Breakwell and to which it was suggested a feeder line could be profitably put in to the CM & DP but this was never more than a nebulous idea.

Still climbing and meandering alongside the Rea the train passed into the Parish of Stottesdon and reached Prescott (originally to be called Oreton) with its platform and siding (5m 25¼ch), having passed the site of an early cotton mill.

After crossing another road at Prescott, the inspection party passed by the confluence of the Farlow Brook and River Rea. The original plans were for the Farlow Brook to be diverted from its channel to join the Rea a short way up the line thereby requiring only one bridge to be built instead of two. However this was not carried out and the remains of the two separate bridges still exist long after the railway has closed. The party, having passed the halfway stage near Day House crossing, arrived at Stottesdon station (6m 58¾ch). Here was the first halting place after Cleobury Town to be given the title of a Station and was similarly equipped with station building, containing a waiting room and a porter's room. A passing loop, cattle dock and end loading facilities were also provided.

From this point onwards, with the exception of odd tracts of land owned by the various local councils, and a small piece owned by the church, the line traversed land belonging to the Burwarton estate of Lord Boyne.

The locomotive's fireman was now working hard as the special continued its relentless climb towards its destination at Ditton Priors and after crossing the river near Duddlewick the railway forsook the banks of the Rea for the valley of its tributary, the Moor Brook, and shortly drew into Aston Botterell where, at 8m 45ch, a platform and siding had been put in to accommodate the local people from Aston Botterell hamlet, Cockshall cottages and the Bold Farm, home of Mr Williamson, co-founder of the Burwarton Coal and Trading Co.

View of the aerial ropeway and pylons on Catherton Common, looking towards Titterstone Clee. Brown Clee is in the centre distance.

Courtesy E. Wall

Stottesdon in 1908, looking towards Cleobury Town with the cattle dock on the left. The station name board displays the original spelling "Stottesden".

W. Atkinson

Burwarton station in 1908, looking towards Cleobury Town.   *W. Atkinson*

A little over a mile further on, the party arrived at Burwarton station, also afforded the same facilities as the other "Stations", and incidentally the last of the four shelters, to remain after the line was closed and lifted, enabling detailed plans to be made from it. The station was situated closer to Charlcotte than the village of Burwarton and its Hall, which had been saddened by the death of Lord Boyne earlier that year. It is a curious fact that it was not originally intended to have a station here at all. Although plans were submitted to Lord Boyne, he disapproved of the idea, suggesting to Mr Foxlee that a private siding for his own use be put in instead (also that trains should stop at all the stations on his estate). We can only speculate that after his death his son viewed the plans with favour and gave his personal permission for the station to be built.

Leaving Burwarton station behind, the Inspecting Officer's train proceeded northwards passing to the east the site of Charlcotte iron furnace dating back to the 18th century and at 10m 38ch drew slowly up to the crossing at Cleobury North Halt where the fireman stepped down to open them.

The village of Cleobury North, of all those served by the railway, had its nucleus centred nearest to the line, a fact that the villagers had already realized whilst the line was being constructed. Objections to the first siting of a station, then to be named Burwarton, (not to be confused with the station which actually did become Burwarton) meant resiting it, a move which caused some concern to both the CM & DP Lt Rly. Directors and the villagers, as the only available local land was Glebe land belonging to the Parish Church of St Peter and St Paul whose rectory overlooked the proposed new site. Only after lengthy negotiations between the Board and the Church Commissioners did they give up just enough land to accommodate the line plus a small platform. This somewhat angered the villagers who drew up and sent a petition to the Board early in 1908 demanding a siding for goods deliveries. Although the Board was sympathetic they could not accede to the request so Cleobury North as it was to become named suffered the indignity of being the only stopping place on the line without a siding or even, at first, the provision of a shelter.

The inspection party carried on away from Cleobury North through the opened pair of white crossing gates, the second of the two sets of protecting gates on the line, and up the 1:60 grade topping the summit just past Kennel crossing, the original site for Burwarton (Cleobury North) Station. The engine crew could now relax as the line levelled off for the run into Ditton Priors. The inspecting party, in the comparative comfort of the ex North London coaches could look out at the dominating outline of the Brown Clee Hill, visible from the left hand windows of the carriages, a landscape scarred by many years of quarrying, and which must have appeared very bleak and forbidding on this cold November day in 1908.

Finally the terminus at Ditton Priors was reached on the level at the western edge of the village about ¼ mile from the centre. Here the party inspected the station area which consisted of the standard CM & DP Lt Rly station building, cattle dock, run round loop and, like Cleobury Town, watering facilities for the locomotives. There was also a rail inter connection from the Abdon incline to sidings behind the main platform building. Here also was a small wooden engine shed housing the Quarry Company's locomotive responsible for working the stone traffic from the bottom of the incline to Ditton Priors yard.

Lieutenant-Colonel Yorke was generally satisfied with what he saw and later, on making his report, stated he had travelled the line which was 12 miles 67 chains long. The flat bottom track was ex LSWR bought secondhand weighing 72lbs per yard and was dog spiked to the sleepers with the assistance of fang bolts and clips, the fang bolts being placed on either side of the rail at the joints and on the outside rail halfway between the joints.

On curves additional fang bolts were used on the outside of the outer rail, these being further supported on the outside by blocks of wood spiked to the sleepers and pressing against the web of the rail. Sleepers were recorded as being 8ft long by 9ins by 4½ins, lying on ballast of broken stone and furnace ashes which, according to the inspector was not of sufficient quantity, and he required this to be made good as quickly as possible.

He also stated that the railway could safely open for passenger traffic, providing that his additional recommendations were duly followed. An increase in the quantity of ballast was called for, and, whilst track and ballast was settling, the speed limit of 25 miles per hour was dropped to 20 mph for the first 6 months. For safety reasons, turnouts and siding operations at the four larger stations had to come into line with the method employed at the unmanned halts and sidings. This entailed changing the large balance levers and padlocks on the turnouts and substituting for them single lever ground frames, using the Annett lock system controlled by the key on the train staff.

He noted and approved the timetable of three mixed trains a day consisting of 8.20 am ex Cleobury Town, 11.10 am and 4.35 pm ex Cleobury Mortimer Junction returning from Ditton Priors at 9.35 am, 3.00 pm and 6.5 pm, the fare being 1/- (5p) single 3rd class, 1/6d (7½p) 1st class.

In a letter to the Board after the inspection, Mr Foxlee recorded that the passenger service commenced later than he had hoped, in fact on Saturday November 21st, 1908 (one day after the date mentioned in a contemporary article about the new line in the April 1909 *Railway Magazine*) and to begin with a curtailed service operated, 9.42 am and 2.30 pm ex Junction to Ditton Priors with 11.20 am and 4.45 pm return to the Junction from Ditton Priors.

So after eight years of frustration, the line had finally opened bringing railway transport to this rural part of Shropshire. The South Shropshire Edwardian Scene would now include an immaculate green saddle tank hauling two equally shiny varnished teak coaches, no doubt with excited faces at the windows and perhaps also a couple of goods vehicles in front of the grey brake van all proceeding at a leisurely pace, destined for the markets at Kidderminster, or, who knows?, a promised trip to London or the Welsh Coast.

The *Bridgnorth Journal* notes in December 1908

At the request of several inhabitants of the district, Mr Morris, the energetic and obliging manager of the Light Railway ran a special passenger train from Ditton Priors to connect with an excursion to Birmingham. The coaches were much admired for their comfort and convenience and the punctuality and smooth running of the train was particularly noted. The special train was very well patronized and great praise is due to the officials for their great care and attention to the passengers.

With a loco prodigiously whistling at every crossing up and down the line, the CM & DP Lt Rly had well and truly opened.

A humorous post card of the day.   *Courtesy Mrs. S. Sutton*

Left Unknown navvy and his typical dwelling.
W. Atkinso

Right CM & DP football team with Cleobury Mortimer Church in the background. Top left, E. Morris, Railway Manager; second from right, T. Dowding; far right, A. Russell.

Courtesy N. Howe

Left . Bott & Stennett staff. Back row: Harry Short, W. Hicks, P.A. Wright, Slen Coe, — Coe. Seated: Mr. Farrant, Walter Atkinson, Alf Russell, Herbert Wilson. On ground: Billy Laws (office boy).
Courtesy N. Howe

CHAPTER SIX

Years before the First World War

THE year of 1909 was entered with great optimism for the railway's future. An immediate boost to this confidence was the increased goods traffic brought about by the opening in February of the Detton Ford-Titterstone Clee aerial ropeway and the sidings used by the Clee Hill Granite Company at Detton Ford. Here wagons were hauled off the CM & DP across the road by horse and then placed under the discharge hoppers at the ropeway's terminus. The stone, having previously been graded from 2½ in to dust, was then dropped by gravity to the waiting wagons below.

Both the Great Western and the Midland Railways used the stone for ballast and open wagons belonging to both companies were amongst those to be seen lined up in the Detton Ford sidings along with those belonging to the Clee Hill Granite Company.

Also in February discussion took place about quotes for uniforms for the staff, one of these being finally approved. New staff appointments were also made, a fireman (no name) was paid 25/- (£1.25p) per week, Mr Jack Strong, (Driver) 36/- (£1.80p) per week, Mr Treacy, (Goods Porter) 25/- per week and Mr F. Cook, (Clerk to the Manager) 15/- (75p) per week.

In the Summer of 1909 the increasing popularity of the connection to Kidderminster market meant that once a month in July, August and September, an additional train was run from Ditton Priors and back. Another special was called for, and run from Burwarton to Cleobury Town leaving at 8.15 pm, after the "Burwarton Industrial, Horticultural and Poultry Society" show on 12th August, 1909, the line carrying 300 extra passengers on the one day!, stretching the resources of the railway to the limit.

In September 1909 it was clear that after a year of operation the ballast was still not in a settled or satisfactory state. In a report, the Permanent Way Inspector, Mr Alfred Wheeler, asked for an extra consignment of ballast to deal with his problems, as a derailment to *Burwarton* earlier in March had been blamed on the bad ballast. However, his request was not met, he being advised to lift "only the slacks" and not try to pack ballast beneath the sleepers beyond the 6ins depth allowed for!

A letter from Mr Stennett to Mr Morris in October 1909 expressing his pleasure that some Billingsley coal had been sent via Stottesdon is a reminder of the fact that there must have been a little disappointment over the failure of the "Stottesdon, Kinlet and Billingsley Light Railway" which Mr Foxlee had set out on plan to connect with a junction at Stottesdon. The coal from the Billingsley Colliery Company's pit near the "Cape of Good Hope" inn on the Bridgnorth to Kinlet road was eventually carried out via the Borle valley and Highley on the GWR Severn Valley line.

The failure of this planned extension was no setback to the financial status of the line, however, for the second half yearly freight figures for 1909 were very encouraging and show how busy the line had been, 32,345 tons having been carried in the 6 months ending 31st December, 1909. A profit of £734 was made on an income of £3,370 after all the hire purchase costs had

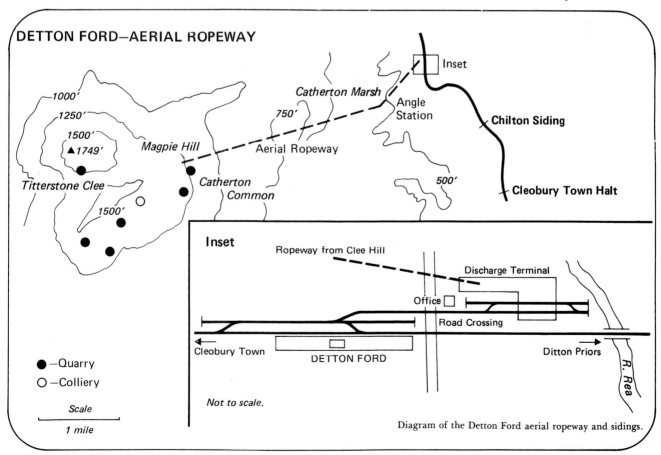

Diagram of the Detton Ford aerial ropeway and sidings.

C.M. + D.P. Lt. Rly.
STATION SHELTER. (BURWARTON)

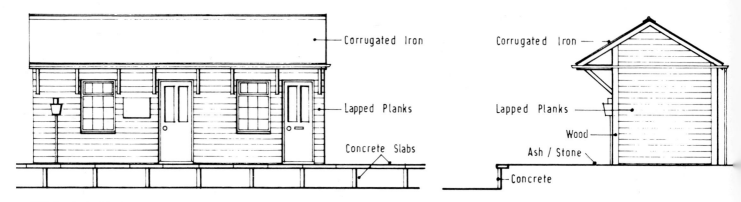

Corrugated Iron

Lapped Planks

Concrete Slabs

Corrugated Iron

Lapped Planks

Wood

Ash / Stone

Concrete

WEST ELEVATION

SCALE: 4mm / 1ft.
SOURCE: Field Measurements.

SOUTH ELEVATION

SCALE: 4mm / 1ft.
SOURCE: Field Measurements.

West and south elevations of the station shelter at Burwarton — a typical CM & DP design.
Courtesy C. Eyre

been paid. Of the 17,240 train miles run that year only 286 were on passenger service, all the remaining mileage was on freight or mixed freight and passenger. Sometimes freight traffic density had been so great that there were wagons waiting to be moved from Detton Ford sidings and trains from Ditton Priors, already consisting of a maximum permitted 12 loaded wagons, could take no more so delays to traffic from the Clee Hill Granite Company occurred as a result.

In 1910 the operating surplus for the year had reached four figures (£1,003) (with 15,000 passengers and 77,000 tons of freight carried) and this was more than doubled in 1911 (£2,214) without additional locomotive mileage.

Early in 1911, the locomotive fitter who was, incidentally, Mr E. Morris's son resigned to join the GWR leaving a problem regarding locomotive maintenance. As a result, arrangements were made with the Great Western Company for repairs to be carried out at their Worcester works. In this year too Mr Bott had now joined his contracting partner Mr Stennett on the CM & DP Lt Rly Board of Directors, where Mr Stennett was now very much the Managing Director of the Railway, for all references and enquiries relating to matters concerning the immediate running of the line were usually made to him personally.

The Burwarton Coal and Trading Company were now finding increased business and in 1911 asked the CM & DP to build a cart weighbridge for them at Cleobury Town station. The Board, in reply to the request, told the Burwarton manager that his company must build one for themselves as the Clee Hill and Abdon Clee Companies had done. One was eventually built, however, being jointly used by the Coal Co. and the Light Railway.

Even in those days there were threats to the supply of coal and the Board had decided, in 1911, to order extra stocks of steam coal from South Wales as a contingency plan against a possible coalminers' strike which was being talked about at the time.

In view of the most successful financial start for the railway, it is not surprising that another, different extension of the railway

northwards was proposed by Mr Foxlee in the early months of 1912. In a memorandum to the Board he gave a selection of possibilities. The first mirrored, to some extent, the abortive Stottesdon, Kinlet and Billingsley Light Railway scheme in that it sought an outlet onto the GWR's Severn Valley Branch. The second involved a link with the LNWR Coalport branch and about 12 miles of steep gradients and engineering problems which would cost a prohibitive sum around the £100,000 mark. The idea favoured by Mr Stennett was Mr Foxlee's third alternative. This was a proposed line extending from Ditton Priors into Corvedale with a stopping place at the village of Weston before entering Upper Corvedale to reach the GWR's Much Wenlock branch at Presthope where it could tap the Lilleshall Companies' limestone traffic.

Although Mr Stennett gave his personal backing, he did not move the rest of the directors to give encouragement for this expansion. The Board had more immediate problems at the time, being greatly concerned over the half expected failure in steam coal supply from South Wales where miners had, by this time, gone on strike. The Board had, as stated earlier, laid in supplies in readiness but there was no way of knowing how long the difficult supply situation would remain and there was also the fear that the GWR would curtail their big regular stone traffic order as one of their own economy measures to save coal.

Alongside the national labour problem, the Board had to consider a wages claim from its own staff which it eventually granted. The new weekly rates dating from June 1912 were recorded as Permanent Way Inspector Wheeler 40/- (£2) per week, Drivers T. Dowding and J. Strong the same, Fireman Howe 28/- 6d (£1.42½p), Foreman Treacy 30/- (£1.50), Guard Teague 30/-, Shunter Bennal and Clerk Cook 25/- (£1.25p), Gangers 22/- (£1.10p), Cleaners 19/- (95p) and finally Platelayers 18/- (90p) per week.

Falling passenger traffic was also giving the Board some concern. Market ticket sales on Wednesdays for the weekly Cleobury Mortimer market had dropped off noticeably and it had become difficult to cover the overall cost of running the passenger service. One suggestion made by the Board was to contact the GWR with a view to buying a secondhand rail-motor from them. Mr Morris duly contacted Mr Ireland of the Great Western who stated that his company might perhaps be willing to dispose of a type which had the tubes arranged crossways instead of longitudinally and was, therefore, inconvenient to the GWR. The CM & DP Lt Rly directors worked out costs of running a rail-motor over the line without a trailer to be, in rough figures, Driver £1.16s (£1.80p), Fireman £1.4s (£1.20p), Conductor £1.4s, Coal £25 per mile, repairs 10/-(50p) per day, at £50 per annum which brought the total running costs of the vehicle to the railway per week to a figure around £8.4s, an amount which the Manager could not guarantee to cover and so the idea was shelved.

Goods traffic was not, in any way, faltering with stone traffic continuing to pay well, the GW and Midland Railways using it in large quantities as ballast.

The Light Railway developed, over the years, a very healthy traffic in items other than stone and coal. Milk was collected along the line, beer was delivered for local public houses, animal food consignments were brought in and flour for the bakers also came by rail. An account book from Mill Farm, Farlow shows how iron arrived at Prescott station for the local blacksmith. A considerable quantity of timber was moved out, and explosives for the Abdon Clee quarries were carried up to Ditton Priors. Fruit and sugar beet were carried away in season, as well as produce coming in for sale at local shops particularly in Ditton Priors, but a warning note was sounded in a comment from the manager, Mr Morris, at a Board meeting when he referred to the number of carters then operating a service out of Cleobury Mortimer carrying to local villages in direct competition with the Light Railway.

One of the most used services was the cattle train special, run on a Thursday to carry stock to and from Kidderminster market. The empty vans started their journey up the line between 5 and 6 am to collect the stock starting back from Ditton Priors about 8 am. The Company then returned unsold or newly bought animals from Cleobury Mortimer at around 9 pm. The service was offered once a month and in August 1912 there was a suggestion from Nock & Joseland, Auctioneers of Kidderminster, that Mr Morris might consider letting these trains run at a new fortnightly Thursday interval during July, August, September and possibly October. Nock & Joseland pointed out in a letter to the Secretary of the Railway that although Mr Morris asked for a guarantee of six trucks per train when the service started in 1909, the twenty two trains run since 1911 averaged 9½ trucks per journey and upon occasions had risen to as high as 18 cattle wagons on one train. Mr Morris's reply asked for a guarantee of 10 trucks per train for the proposed service but the auctioneers felt this rather high and returned with an offer of 8 trucks per train reminding Mr Morris that he was losing a little trade for the line each fortnight that farmers were forced to look for alternative transport and stating that they were in full expectation of being well above their suggested guarantee figure. The outcome was that the Railway agreed to try the fortnightly cattle truck service until October of that year although it is not clear whose guarantee figures were applied.

Direct access to the village from Cleobury Town Station had been improved by now with a bridge across the Rea by the Paper Mill, the Railway Board donating 2 guineas to help with the cost of construction, but the arrangements provided for a service to Chilton were not quite working out according to plan. Mrs Tomkinson, who lived at Chilton, had complained about a train not stopping, the Board having agreed to stop all trains at Chilton platform when requested to do so by Mrs Tomkinson. However Mrs Tomkinson wished to keep to the letter of the original agreement and have all the trains stop regardless of request, but a note was returned to her saying that this condition could not be met, although Mrs Tomkinson could still continue to have any train stopped on giving prior notice to the manager. There is no more record of correspondence following this so the matter may have rested there. One railwayman remembers getting into trouble, however, for failing to deliver personally to the door a package received by train, handing it instead to one of Mrs Tomkinson's employees to carry to the house.

Ditton Priors station in 1907, with original short platform and twin water tanks. One of these was provided for the Abdon Clee Quarry Co., whose sidings were situated between the station shelter and the navvy accommodation huts, connecting at the far end of the platform. The cattle dock can be seen in the right background. Note the original point levers.

W. Atkinson

CHAPTER SEVEN

1914-1922

U P until 1914, watering the locos had been carried out from small wooden tanks which Bott and Stennett's workmen had erected at both Cleobury Town and Ditton Priors. Now, it was thought by the Manager, a bigger capacity tank should be provided at Cleobury Town. After trying W. Richards and Son without any useful result, the GWR were approached to find out if they had any second hand umbrella water columns available. A new one at the time cost £100 exclusive of site erection and Mr Stennett wondered if the current arrangements could be kept going for a while, for as he said at the time "it is easy enough to spend money but very hard to get it". However, the GWR must have had a bargain available for shortly afterwards the buying was authorised of, not one, but two columns and these were to be delivered free of charge to Cleobury Mortimer. One, of 2,000 gallons capacity, went to Cleobury Town and the other of 1,000 gallons capacity, to Ditton Priors, the cost being £60 and £40 respectively.

In April 1914 there was recorded a salary increase for Manager, Mr Morris from £225 per annum to £250 per annum and, in addition, a bonus equal to 1½% on the realised profits of the Railway.

In August the First World War broke out and the Government took control of all railways in Britain. This control was exercised through a Railway Executive Committee which Mr Stennett attended but there was little immediate effect on the day to day running of the Light Railway. The Directors made a minuted reference to the outbreak of the War, expressing their confident opinion, like others in the country, "that it would all be over by Christmas".

By now, according to Mr Morris, the locomotives were in need of repair although Mr Stennett disagreed with this observation. Someone, he said, from the GWR should come across from Worcester and give an independent opinion about the condition of the tyres which was the problem in question. It was the supposed bad state of these which was blamed by Mr Morris for a recent derailment of a light loco. Mr Stennett reminded Mr Morris that the locos ran four years from new up until 1912 when £126.9.6 (£126.47½p) and £130 was paid per loco for the wheels to be turned up. Mr Stennett considered that the wheels should last in good condition as long as they had done before, not half as long! He was of the opinion that the loco came off the rails because the points were not set properly and for no other reason and that the wheels ought to be left for another two years. Eventually, however, Mr Stennett conceded the argument and *Burwarton* left for Worcester to have its tyres turned.

From 1915 onwards throughout the war the demand for dhustone began to increase. It was required by the military amongst other new customers and a regular supply was transported to Aldershot for the duration of the war. In fact, local regular customers like Bridgnorth R.D.C. were required to give preference to the military. All fuel resources had to be

Concrete railway offices at Cleobury Town built on post panel principle by the Abdon Quarry Company, c1919.   *Authors' Collection*

conserved and so there were times when the buckets of the Detton aerial ropeway transported coal slack from the old, previously idle, Clee Hill pits down to the railway instead of their usual stone with female labour being brought in to help with the loading. Manpower on the railway was not depleted, however, the full staff being maintained, in spite of growing demands throughout Britain for re-inforcements from the fronts in Europe. There was now an urgent need for additional wagons to cope with the upsurge of demand for stone. Abdon Clee Quarry Co ordered 25 new wagons on hire purchase from the British Wagon Company in June 1915 but Mr Cross, the Quarry Manager, found this number still insufficient and, only a month later, in July another 50 were bought second hand on seven years hire purchase at £12.15s (£12.75p) per wagon per year.

There was a reference at this time in a report from the Permanent Way Foreman, concerning a broken rail and it is of interest in the fact that the breakage is attributed to "the Great Western engine heavier than ours which has been working the traffic", and later advice was given by the Board to "use the Great Western as much as possible but keep them clear of management in any shape or form". The engine concerned was "850" class 0-6-0PT No. 2001 on wartime loan to the CM & DP from Kidderminster in November 1914 to May 1915.

All the time since 1908 the wooden engine shed at Cleobury Town had served the railway and had obviously now far outlived its usefulness since Mr Morris had been making repeated requests for its replacement since 1909, on the grounds that it was not high enough for wheel dropping to take place with the locomotive inside, this having to be done outside.

In early 1915, Mr Stennett wrote to Lord Boyne saying that the Board would have to give Mr Morris a new shed before long and to this end some advice about plans and costs of a new shed had already been sought from the well known Colonel Stephens in his capacity as adviser to Light Railways. A long correspondence was entered into but nothing substantial came from it.

It happened that a major development was taking place of a new industry sited alongside the railway at Ditton Priors under the general direction of Mr Hamish Cross of the Abdon Clee Stone Quarry Company. The idea was to prefabricate buildings using a post and panel principle in a concrete and dhustone mix of various proportions. The system was intended for use in new housing developments, industrial and farm buildings. The dwelling houses constructed using this method had two walls interspaced by an insulating cavity.

The Quarry manager had a bungalow built for himself at "Oldfield", Ditton Priors as if to emphasise his own confidence in the system. Similarly a new village hall was built at Ditton Priors and the Burwarton estate used the idea in many farm buildings. The Board's suggestion was to build a new loco shed using this local material and method and the illustration taken from the firm's catalogue shows the Town shed as new. The order was put in hand to Mr Cross in 1915 at a cost of £600 but only after suspicions about the lack of strength of the concrete had been removed, Mr Cross quoting similar work done by him as far away as Salisbury, LSWR shed. The plans were looked at by no one less than Mr G.J. Churchward of the GWR who made suggestions regarding minimum height and length pointing out the need for a fitter's cabin. Mr Morris however, had to wait a further two years before he could get his two locos rehoused due to delays in the erection of the concrete shed.

1916 saw increase in freight traffic other than stone, for Lord Boyne's estate sent a consignment of round timber totalling an estimated 4,000 trees in that year, details of which were arranged through Mr Pierce of the Burwarton Estate. In a letter to the Railway's secretary from Mr Caryl Roberts of the Manor House, Cleobury Mortimer there is a reference to the "very pleasing figures in the last report" and Mr Stennett was able to report to Mr T. Hamilton-Russell that the CM & DP finances were very satisfactory but added that he wished he could say the same about Abdon Clee. It appears that, as on its giant railway neighbour, the War had not put a stop to the public travelling

The Abdon Quarry Company's concrete works at Ditton Priors. Mixing sheds on the right and "Railway Cottages" in the background. View taken c1917.

Authors' Collection

The stacking ground at the concrete works, showing 2ft gauge track with bogie. A wooden mould can be seen in the foreground.
Authors' Collection

Another view of the stacking ground. The Abdon Quarry Co.'s shed and locomotive are visible in the middle distance.
Authors' Collection

in fact the reverse had happened. Mr Roberts had come to the defence of Cleobury Mortimer's traders because there was, at this time, a petition being raised by farmers at the Ditton Priors end of the line who wanted Wednesday's special passenger train services (Cleobury Mortimer's market day) altered to a Thursday (Kidderminster's day). Mr Roberts expressed his personal opposition to this unless the Company could run special services on both days. For, as he concludes in a letter, "the line was expressly built to develop this place (Cleobury Mortimer) and district and not to enrich the shopkeepers of Kidderminster".

At a later Board meeting, it was agreed to try the extra Thursday market special subject to the costs being met by February 1917. The additional passenger services were under particular scrutiny by Mr Stennett and the Board because of the controls now being imposed on passenger traffic by the wartime Government. The continuation of the additional working was considered under every possible condition but the Board found it impracticable to do anything other than cancel it. "A matter", reported Mr Stennett, "that has caused the most extreme regret to the Board because the request was generally supported and by the most influential residents". "But" he added, "the case is not an isolated one, as other people are suffering due to the war and control by the Government.

"As soon as the directors assume control again, the desired arrangements can be made".

At the same meeting it was recorded that some directors had purchased freehold land at Ditton Priors to build on, which, they suggested, would benefit the Railway by bringing extra passengers. Again at the same February meeting it was reported that the new engine shed was almost finished, the remaining work being the buffer stop. With the opening of the new shed in May 1917, another improved amenity was provided for the efficient running of the railway. Maintenance was eased and coaling the locos off a stand which could be illuminated by a lamp supported on an Abdon Clee concrete standard was that much less of a problem than before.

The 'post and panel' system reinforced concrete from Ditton Priors was used again for a new office at Cleobury Town put in hand in 1917 and for 8' x 6' platform shelters at Detton Ford and Cleobury North, the latter in response to public demand put forward by Mr Claude Hamilton-Russell.

The Management were actively planning for the end of the war (and of Government Control) in 1917 with a new passenger timetable drawn up by Mr Morris at Mr Stennett's request. Mr Morris again favoured the idea of a railmotor. Mr Stennett noted that it would be possible to operate such a vehicle without signalling the Railway but added as a realistic afterthought "if we can induce someone to make us a present of it."

The war ended with a pay rise for the staff but with William Stennett reported gravely ill. The CM & DP like many facets of Britain and its railways was never the same again afterwards. The bringing together of railway workers under one single Government control had allowed true comparison of wages and working conditions to be made. The eight hour working day and a standard wage for the job throughout the country were two important changes which now affected railway management after the war and it was generally found that working expenses in 1919 had more than doubled those operating in 1913 with the extra cost of fuel and materials, let alone rates and taxes. In the last month of 1918, William Stennett died having ably directed the Company in peace and war. His former partner Mr Bott now took over the role of Managing Director as the Company moved back into peace time operation.

The year of 1919 was a formative time for the CM & DP Lt Rly for it did not pass back into local control as had been expected because the Ministry of Transport Act established the Ministry and gave the Government control of Britain's railways for two more years pending a definite policy statement about their future. Freight rates were increased, passenger fares were also increased as much as 75% above those of 1917 and the small lanes of the Rea Valley became more used to the sound of the internal combustion engine delivering the goods. That was not all. The Railway Unions enforced their wage demands with a strike which was settled quickly but added more money to the wages bill. There is little reference to the 1919 labour situation on the Cleobury line but it must have had its effect because the Abdon Clee Quarry Company were requested by letter to phone Mr Morris daily "when everything would be done to keep the train service running".

Two more railway employees' cottages were built in concrete post and panel at Cleobury Town in 1919 just below the Bridgnorth road crossing site. Connection with the GWR management was continued after the war by the suggestion to them that the annual permanent way inspection be done by one of their engineers along with the Light Railway's own engineer, Mr. Foxlee. Also *Burwarton* and *Cleobury* in turn went away to Worcester for repairs in 1919. The rather belated peace-

Timetable 21st June, 1915 and until further notice					
Weekdays only, mixed trains Tues & Thurs excepted					
UP				**DOWN**	
	(A)	(B)		(C)	(D)
Ditton Priors	dep 11.05 am	dep 4.10 pm	Cleobury Mortimer Jn.	dep 9.19 am	dep 2.25 pm
Burwarton	dep 11.20 am	dep 4.24 pm	Cleobury Town	arr 9.30 am	arr 2.38 pm
Stottesdon	dep 11.34 am	dep 4.38 pm		dep 9.35 am	dep 2.45 pm
Cleobury Town	arr 12.05 pm	arr 5.15 pm	Stottesdon	dep 10.00 am	dep 3.10 pm
	dep 12.06 pm		Burwarton	dep 10.15 am	dep 3.25 pm
Cleobury Mortimer Jn.	arr 12.22 pm		Ditton Priors	dep 10.33 am	arr 3.45 pm

Notes
A. Mon & Wed only, calling Aston Botterell & Prescott sidings if required on Wednesdays.
B. Wed, Fri & Sat only & will not pick up or set down at sidings.
C. Mon & Wed only.
D. Wed, Fri & Sat only.

Cleobury Town locomotive shed seen shortly after construction in 1917.

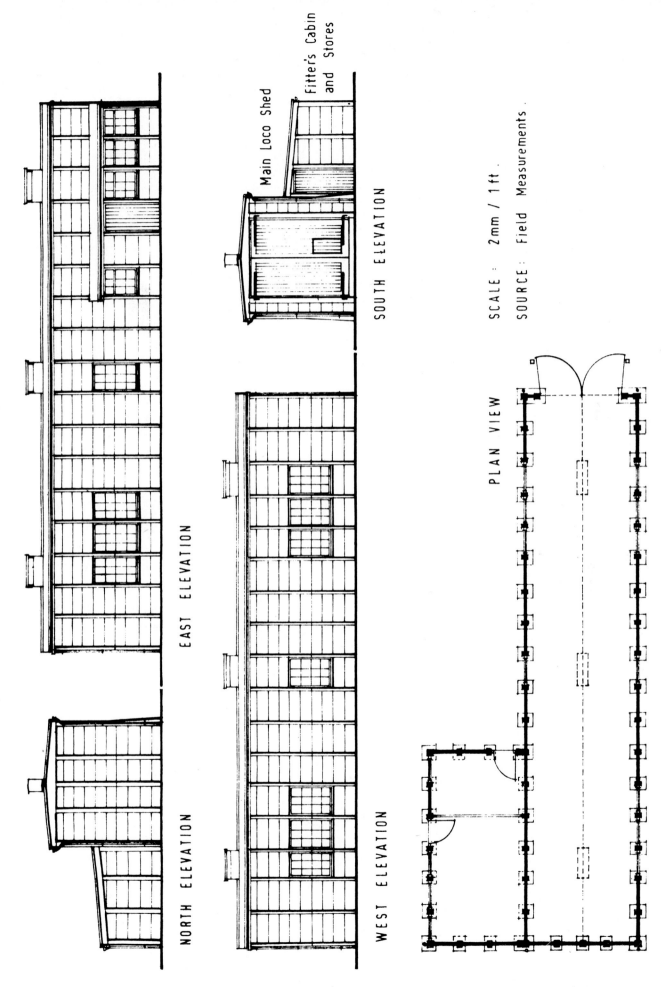

C.M.+D.P. Lt: Rly: ENGINE SHED. (CLEUBURY TOWN)

EAST ELEVATION

NORTH ELEVATION

Main Loco Shed

Fitter's Cabin and Stores

SOUTH ELEVATION

WEST ELEVATION

PLAN VIEW

SCALE : 2mm / 1ft.

SOURCE : Field Measurements .

Plan and elevations of the CM & DP locomotive shed at Cleobury Town.

Courtesy C. Eyre

A piece of the original flat bottom rail with dogs and spike.

Authors' Collection, courtesy E. Wall

The last CM & DP timetable, issued at the time of the Grouping.
L&GRP

Cleobury Mortimer & Ditton Priors Light Railway.

Taken over by Great Western Rly - June 1922

TIME TABLE

NOVEMBER 2nd, 1921, and until further notice

WEEK DAYS ONLY.—MIXED TRAINS.

TUESDAYS AND THURSDAYS EXCEPTED.

UP.			A	B	C
			A.M.	P.M.	P.M.
DITTON PRIORS	...	dep.	11 0	12 30	3 50
Cleobury North Crossing	...	pass	D	D	
BURWARTON	...	dep.	11 15	12 45	4 0
Aston Botterell Siding	...	pass	D		
STOTTESDON	...	dep.	11 30	1 0	4 10
Prescott Siding	...	pass	D	D	
Detton Ford Siding	...	"	D	D	
Chilton Siding	...	"	D	D	
CLEOBURY TOWN	...	arr.	12 5	1 29	4 45
" "	...	dep.	12 6	1 30	
CLEOBURY MORTIMER JUNC.	arr.		12 20	1 45	

DOWN.			A	B	C
			A.M.	A.M.	P.M.
CLEOBURY MORTIMER JUNC.	dep.		9 18	10 55	2 30
CLEOBURY TOWN	...	arr.	9 28	11 5	2 40
" "	...	dep.	9 30	11 7	2 45
Chilton Siding	...	pass	D	D	
Detton Ford Siding	...	"	D	D	D
Prescott Siding	...	"	D	D	D
STOTTESDON	...	dep.	9 55	11 30	3 5
Aston Botterell Siding	...	pass	D	D	
BURWARTON	...	dep.	10 13	11 45	3 20
Cleobury North Crossing	...	pass	D	D	
DITTON PRIORS	...	arr.	10 30	12 0	3 35

A Will run on Mondays, Wednesdays, and Saturdays only. Every exertion will be made for the 11.0 a.m. train from Ditton Priors to connect with the Great Western Company's train due to leave Cleobury Mortimer Junction at 12.38 p.m., but the Company cannot be responsible for any delay caused through late arrival.

B Will run on Fridays only.

C Will run on Wednesdays and Saturdays only.

D Calls if required.

Trains will not run on Christmas Day or Good Friday.

The Company do not guarantee that the trains shall start or arrive at the times printed, and liability cannot be accepted for any delay caused through late running of the trains.

E. J. MORRIS, General Manager

Cleobury Mortimer, October 20th, 1921.

H. G. PERKINS, PRINTER, LOAD STREET, BEWDLEY.

celebrations at Ditton Priors also took place later in the year under the guidance of Abdon Clee Quarry managing director Mr Cross when the employees and the rest of the parish were treated to a "substantial tea".

The Light Railway continued to operate in this uncertain period with success and increased activity for in terms of mileage run, figures show:—

	1919	1920
Coaching	4,220	4,491
Freight	8,151	9,180

and an overall increase including shunting and assisting movements of 14,738 miles run in 1919 to 18,099 in 1920. It would appear also that the maximum load of 12 loaded trucks had been largely ignored during the war and by now 20 loaded wagons were being hauled up the 1:60 gradients.

The CM & DP was still looking after its employees' accommodation for in 1921 there is a record of the purchase of Redthorne House, Cleobury Mortimer for Mr Morris. In this year also the fate of the independent existence of the railway was sealed when the Government passed the Railways Act which became law on 19th August, 1921. The principle of this Act was to group the railways of Britain into only four companies by a process of amalgamation or absorption. The Great Western Railway was the only one to retain its former title and it was into this neighbouring company that the CM & DP Lt Rly was absorbed as a subsidiary. The Board at the time was recorded, still maintaining Boyne family connections with Hon. Eustace S. Hamilton-Russell as Chairman and with R.L. Caryl Roberts the only member remaining on the Board from the pioneering days of fourteen years before. Mr Frank Butcher was secretary then and it was his job to sign the final letter under the title of the Light Railway. It was addressed by the Secretary of the GWR, Paddington Station and dated 25th May, 1922 and in it was enclosed the two keys to the seal of the CM & DP Lt Rly. The line, a little over 12 miles, had been added to the 3,000 plus already worked by the Great Western Railway.

bove *Cleobury*, at Cleobury Mortimer, waits to start with the 9.15 am mixed ‑ain to Ditton Priors on 1st May, 1920.

Ken Nunn/LCGB

Below *Cleobury* coaling off the stage placed opposite the locomotive shed at Cleobury Town. 1st May, 1920.

Ken Nunn/LCGB

Cleobury has arrived at Ditton Priors with the 9.15 am mixed from Cleobury Mortimer. 1st May, 1920.

Above Cleobury arriving at Cleobury Town on the 2.25 pm mixed train to
Ditton Priors on 1st May, 1920.

Ken Nunn/LCGB

Below On the same day, *Cleobury* starts the 2.25 pm mixed to Ditton Priors
away from Cleobury Town.

Ken Nunn/LCGB

Cleobury has run round its train and prepares to leave Ditton Priors with the 11.15 am mixed to Cleobury Mortimer, which includes a heavy load of stone. 1st May, 1920.

Ken Nunn/LCGB

Above Form for a vote by proxy for the Special General Meeting of the
CM & DP Board on 4th April, 1922.

PRO

Top Right Correspondence to Cleobury Mortimer & Ditton Priors Light
Railway shareholders relating to the Grouping.

PRO

Right Letter to Felix Pole, General Manager of the Great Western Railway,
confirming acceptance by the CM & DP Board to absorption.

PRO

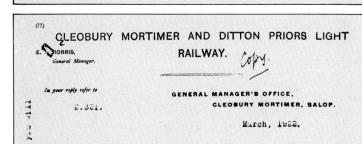

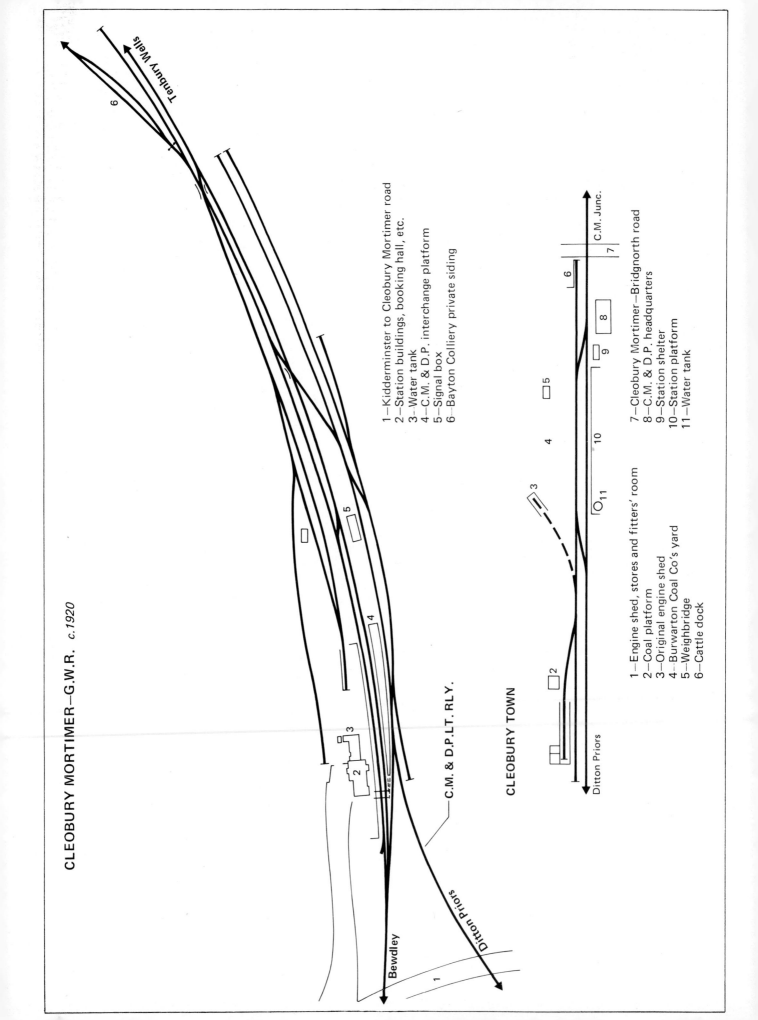

CLEOBURY MORTIMER—G.W.R. *c.1920*

Tenbury Wells

Bewdley

Ditton Priors

C.M. & D.P.LT. RLY.

1—Kidderminster to Cleobury Mortimer road
2—Station buildings, booking hall, etc.
3—Water tank
4—C.M. & D.P. interchange platform
5—Signal box
6—Bayton Colliery private siding

CLEOBURY TOWN

Ditton Priors

C.M. Junc.

1—Engine shed, stores and fitters' room
2—Coal platform
3—Original engine shed
4—Burwarton Coal Co's yard
5—Weighbridge
6—Cattle dock

7—Cleobury Mortimer—Bridgnorth road
8—C.M. & D.P. headquarters
9—Station shelter
10—Station platform
11—Water tank

CHAPTER EIGHT

1922-1938

AT the absorption Mr Felix Pole, General Manager of the GWR sent word that all current staff on the CM & DP Lt Rly would be transferred to the Great Western under conditions no less favourable than they presently enjoyed and that all pension rights were to be honoured.

Shareholders received an exchange for GWR shares and the directors were awarded compensation for loss of office on the basis of four years' fees at £100 per annum, the money to be found from the Light Railway's final assets.

One of the first things that the Great Western Civil Engineers did was to bring the standard of track up to their own. Mr E. Wall of Oreton was one of the platelaying gang at this time and worked alongside Messrs George Thomason, Arthur and George

Priors station had been lengthened at some stage and it could well have coincided with these other platform alterations.

At Abdon, the dhustone was still in good demand, the prefabricated concrete works having a valuable order to build estates of houses near Wolverhampton and Neasden, North London using their post and panel method. This system showed its advantages over conventional building in 1927 when, following a disastrous dam burst near Dolgarrog in North Wales, Abdon prefabricated houses were quickly built to rehouse the homeless families. In addition two tar making plants had been established, one on top of Abdon Clee and a second at the lower end of the incline where the line entered Ditton Priors yard. Road surfacing tests using a tar blended with

Cleobury at Cleobury Mortimer with GWR fittings — including chimney, non-standard safety valve bonnet, tool box, lamp irons and buffers, but with the old lining still showing in places.

M.D. England

Lloyd, Charlie Corfield and Gerry Jordan. Mr Wall recalls how the new owners put plates under some rail joints to give added strength and in many places replaced the old fishplates. The line had been prone to become out of gauge on the tight curves so some of these were immediately relaid by the GWR replacing flat bottom with keyed bullhead rail. At this time some of the turnouts were relaid in a similar manner and the original massive pitch-pine stop blocks were now replaced by standard metal GWR types. The height of platforms along the line were raised by the GWR with the exception of Chilton which remained as it was. A new top edge was made to platforms using concrete slabs made at Ditton Priors, and the platform front faces were slabbed with concrete as well. The platform at Ditton

dhustone had been conducted by the Roads and Bridges Department of Shropshire County Council as long ago as 1912 and these mixtures were now being more widely used throughout the county.

The three Abdon Quarry steam locomotives were still in constant use, *Trent* remaining on top of the incline at the crushing plant with either *Fleetwood* or *Kingswood* working below in Ditton Priors yard. *Fleetwood* had been away for a time during the war for repairs to her firebox. She was due to go back to Hudswell, Clarke's but was sent instead to Heenan and Froude of Worcester where a new firebox was fitted. This locomotive was never quite the same again, however, and suffered from leaky tubes ever after due to the holes in the

Above Cleobury, with a train of four-wheeled Great Western stock, climbing the 1 in 60 gradient through Coach Road Coppice just outside Cleobury Mortimer in 1929.

M.D. England

Below Cleobury at Worcester, showing the first stages of "Great Western-ization": new smokebox, upward extension of bunker, protective bars on rear cab lookouts and cab shutters, but still retaining original buffers.

Real Photographs

firebox tubeplate being slightly bigger than in the smokebox.

The steam engine on top of Abdon had been joined, in 1918, by two, four wheeled petrol engined, Motor Rail Ltd vehicles Nos. 848 and 1029. These two also had War Department Light Railway Nos. 2569 and 2750 as they were supplied via the war-time Railway Executive. They were used on the 2ft gauge line which fed the tipper wagons to the crushing plant and there was also a similar motor rail vehicle used on the short narrow gauge line in the concrete works down at Ditton Priors. These small engines were nicknamed "whizz-bangs" by the quarry staff because of the persistent noise of their backfiring. They were intended, in the quarry at least, to replace the horses but, in fact, often proved rather less reliable.

In the years following the war many farmers in the Ditton Priors area were keen to expand their milk production and to use the branch line as an outlet. With this kind of development in mind, in February 1923, the Bridgnorth branch of the N.F.U. met at the "Howard Arms", Ditton Priors with Mr T. Miller of the GWR in attendance. The farmers wanted the Great Western to run an early morning milk train (to connect at Cleobury Mortimer with a Birmingham train) leaving Ditton Priors at 8 am in the summer and 10 am in the winter. This train it was suggested, could replace the 11.10 a.m., ex Ditton Priors which was poorly supported. Mr Miller promised the N.F.U. branch chairman, Mr W. Williamson, that he would look into the matter but doubted if a special milk train could be run by the GWR without guarantees. To the suggestion at the meeting that an engine shed be provided at Ditton Priors for stabling a loco to work the milk special, Mr Miller was at pains to make it clear that this was impossible. It is not recorded what became of the farmer's request although it is known that in the 1930s milk was collected in a van attached to the "Cleobury College" school special which ran down the branch at a suitably early time.

As a sign of the changing times, the GWR's representative was tackled, at the same meeting, about his Company's high carriage rates for the transport of goods and it was pointed out to him that the Railway was losing some of its traffic to large lorries which were delivering to Ditton Priors at cheaper rates than the GWR.

The Clee Hill Granite sidings at Detton Ford were back to normal working and in addition after the war a small concrete block manufacturing plant was set up close to the terminal using the fine dhustone dust (as at Ditton Priors) as one ingredient. Doddington Lodge then the home of Captain Roberts, Clee Hill Granite Company's director, was extended using these blocks but a shortage of available water, even though the River Rea was close by, prevented the expected expansion of this project. In a period of national and local unemployment when Billingsley Colliery closed and left 200 men unemployed in 1921, Detton Ford aerial ropeway provided a useful source of local employment above all else.

Employed at Detton Ford in this period were the oilers, the men who climbed the trestles in all weathers to keep the bearings and other moving parts lubricated (Messrs Ben Crowther, Tom Wall, Archie Webb, Tom Gilson, George Breakwell and Sam Bishop). At the angle station where the direction of the ropeway was changed were Sam Morris and Albert Sutton whilst Mr Sam Pugh was employed to watch the rope in the "Bogs" area of Catherton Common. The ropeway steam engine required a driver and he was for one period Mr Ben Cleeton. Drivers of the crushing plant engine were Messrs Ted Cleeton and Tom Webb. Foreman at Detton Ford was Mr Chidley and then Mr Bill Price whilst the list of employees at the discharge terminal included Messrs Edwin Martin, Tom Burton, Tom Duce, Bert Key, Bill George, Harry Gilson, G. Broome whilst Tom Breakwell had been trained as a rope splicer and Mr Arthur Lewis worked the shunting horse. In the office Mr Bayfield was clerk and the quantity of jobs provided by the ropeway at this time can be clearly seen from this list of the work force.

Angle station on the aerial ropeway taking dhustone down to Detton Ford. This changed the direction of the ropeway on Catherton Marsh.   *Authors' Collection*

At Burwarton station there was post war development. The Burwarton Industrial, Horticultural and Poultry Society had two huts placed opposite the railway platform where sale of animal feeds delivered by rail was managed by Mr Robert Green under a co-operative scheme organised by local Burwarton people including Mr Lloyd, Major Morgan, Mr W. Williamson, Miss Florence Hamilton-Russell and Mr Kirby. A small coal wharf was established alongside the line at Burwarton Station by Mr Frank Jones who also ran the first local bus around the villages of the Boyne estate.

Under the GWR, Cleobury Town shed became a sub shed to Kidderminster (KDR) and was given the code number 65. Usually only one engine was kept at the Town shed, mainly on a weekly basis, the other engine remaining at Kidderminster which had become responsible for the maintenance of both branch locos. The engine currently stationed at Cleobury would run light each week-end to Kidderminster for boiler washouts and repairs and was exchanged for the other branch engine which would then return to the Town to take up its duties.

The train staff, under the CM & DP Lt Rly, had been kept at the offices at Cleobury Town but was now held in Cleobury Mortimer signal box. If however the branch engine was stabled at Cleobury Town overnight it was locked in the locomotive's toolbox. There were other alterations in running the line brought in by the GWR, although the CM & DP had used the GWR's rule book under their own cover. Trains due to stop at Chilton were now to be arranged through the Station Master at Cleobury Mortimer. When trains running towards Cleobury Mortimer were required to stop at Chilton, sufficient notice had to be given to the trainman to enable the load to be regulated to avoid the risk of failing to restart the train up the bank towards the Town. At Prescott and Aston Botterell sidings, vehicles were only to be picked up or put off by down trains. Shunting at Detton Ford had to be protected by the Guard who was to satisfy himself that the train movements could be carried out across the road in safety and he had to remain on the crossing and exhibit a danger signal to users of the roadway. When shunting was being done at Detton Ford by mixed trains in the up (Cleobury Mortimer) direction, coaches were banned from being taken into the Clee Hill Granite Co sidings and here a red peg was sited at a point beyond which the train engine could not pass i.e. across the weighbridge. A similar red peg was used to stop GWR engines passing into Abdon Clee Company's siding at Ditton Priors. Fouling of road crossings had always been avoided but it was accepted by the Great Western that this was likely to happen at Wyre Common Crossing when freight or mixed trains stopped at the incline board to pin down brakes before descent down to Cleobury Mortimer. Under the GWR, the front guard of a mixed train during darkness or foggy weather, if foul of crossing, had to apply his brakes whilst the rear guard stood on the upside of the crossing showing a red light along the road. The driver was then instructed to draw the whole train clear and stop again for the rear guard to board the train. At Cleobury North Crossing a gate attendant, Mrs Bromley, was employed by the GWR and the gates here and at Cleobury Town were locked after the passage of trains. To protect the gated crossings in foggy weather, detonators were placed 10 yards apart by a fogman, ¼ mile either side of Cleobury Town or Cleobury North gates. Instructions for other crossings in fog were for the driver to sound the whistle and be prepared to stop.

The Great Western Railway's Chief Mechanical Engineer had 925 engines added to his motive power at the grouping of the constituent and subsidiary companies into the "new" GWR and although the Railways Act came into force on 1st January, 1922

it was not until the four weeks ending 13th August, 1922 that CM & DP Nos. 1734 and 1735 were added to GWR stock. In between times a renumbering scheme had been worked out and 1735 *Cleobury* became GWR No. 28 and 1734 *Burwarton* became No. 29. The C.M.E.'s department looked at the capabilities of all the locomotives that it had inherited and decided that its new numbers 28 and 29 were good for a few more years wear and worth rebuilding. *Cleobury* was the first of the pair to visit Swindon works, booked for repair on 7th September, 1922 and not returned to traffic until April 1923. Whilst she was away "850" class 0-6-0ST No. 1948 and 0-6-0PT No. 1970 were sent from Kidderminster to work the branch; No. 1970 from 31st August to 5th November, 1922 and No. 1948 from 18th October to 3rd December, 1922.

In the original Manning, Wardle condition, Swindon gave No. 28 the GWR Diagram No. A 101. Then in its altered state it was allocated Diagram B 7. Internally it was given smaller dimension tubes and a new inside firebox. Externally it lost its travelling jack from the position on the running board and had a GWR parallel chimney fitted. The injector was altered and the standard GWR lamp irons and tool boxes were fitted.

As well as the locos the rest of the Light Railway rolling stock, minus one wagon scrapped earlier, was absorbed by the GWR. The brake third coach No. 3, and the composite No. 4 were renumbered 4264 and 5344 respectively at Swindon during the week ending 19th November, 1922 when they were weighed at 9 tons 1 cwt and 9 tons 13 cwt respectively. Only one wagon had its renumbering completed in 1922 and that was No. 2 which became 34231 at Worcester in December 1922. Other ex Light Railway wagons were withdrawn by the GWR in 1922 without being renumbered (see appendix, page 112).

Burwarton was the first loco to leave for rebuilding at Swindon in 1923 and, although not recorded, it is most likely that deputy engines were working the branch, for *Cleobury* was also at Swindon for four months and *Burwarton* the entire year. When it returned rebuilt as a pannier tank in 1924 No. 29 had been made capable of steam heating so it was natural that the branch carriages should be also adapted and Brake third 4264 (ex CM & DP No. 3) was fitted with heating apparatus in September 1923 whilst 4263 (ex No. 1) followed with this process in March 1924. Presumably this also applied to the two composites but this fact is not recorded in the GWR coach register.

By the end of 1924 all the ex CM & DP wagons that were seen fit to continue in revenue service had been renumbered and withdrawal of most of the 1912 batch of British Wagon Company 8ft wheelbase open wagons was complete. The two goods brakes had been renumbered at Worcester and returned for continued useful service on the branch.

In 1924 the wooden engine shed on top of Abdon Clee that normally housed the quarry shunting engine was burnt to the ground with *Trent* inside it. The engine was damaged and sent back to its makers but then returned later in the year to be housed in a new shed constructed of fireproof dhustone! In June 1925 *Cleobury* spent nearly a month at Worcester works when the process of 'Great Westernization' of the ex CM & DP locomotive continued during a medium heavy repair. A Great Western brass safety valve bonnet was fitted, the buffers front and rear were altered to GW pattern and the coal bunker was extended upwards which necessitated the fitting of protective bars across the rear spectacles to prevent falling coal damaging the glass.

By the first months of 1926 the four ex North London Railway coaches, apparently without further repaint or repair, had been withdrawn and replaced by GWR gas lit four wheeled

Left Burwarton, as Great Western Railway No. 29, after rebuilding in 1924.
D. Rouse Collection

Below GWR fares list for the Cleobury Mortimer — Ditton Priors branch, issued in 1928.
J. Pritchett Collection

GREAT WESTERN RAILWAY.

ORDINARY SINGLE FARES—First and Third Class.

TICKETS WILL BE ISSUED ON THE TRAIN

FROM	TO: Cleobury Mortimer		Cleobury Town Halt		Chilton Siding		Detton Ford Siding		Prescott Siding		Stottesdon Halt		Aston Botterell Siding		Burwarton Halt		Cleobury N. Crossing		Ditton Priors Halt	
	1st s. d.	3rd s. d.	1st s. d.	3rd s. d.	1st s. d.	3rd s. d.	1st s. d.	3rd s. d.	1st s. d.	3rd s. d.	1st s. d.	3rd s. d.	1st s. d.	3rd s. d.	1st s. d.	3rd s. d.	1st s. d.	3rd s. d.	1st s. d.	3rd s. d.
Cleobury Mortimer	—	—	5	3	7½	4½	11½	7	1 2	8½	1 6	10½	1 11	1 2	2 0	1 3	2 3	1 4	2 5	1 6
Cleobury Town Halt	5	3	—	—	2½	1½	6½	4	9	5½	1 1	7½	1 6	10½	1 7	11½	1 10	1 1	2 1	1 3
Chilton Siding ..	7½	4½	2½	1½	—	—	4	2½	6½	4	10	6	1 3	9	1 5	10	1 8	1 0	2 0	1 3
Detton Ford Siding	11½	7	6½	4	4	2½	—	—	2½	1½	6½	4	11½	7	1 1	7½	1 5	10	1 8	1 0
Prescott Siding ..	1 2	8½	9	5½	6½	4	2½	1½	—	—	4	2½	9	5½	11	6½	1 2	8½	1 6	10½
Stottesdon Halt ..	1 6	10½	1 1	7½	10	6	6½	4	4	2½	—	—	5	3	7½	4½	10	6	1 2	8½
Aston Botterell Siding	1 11	1 2	1 6	10½	1 3	9	11½	7	9	5½	5	3	—	—	2½	1½	5	3	9	5½
Burwarton Halt ..	2 0	1 3	1 7	11½	1 5	10	1 1	7½	11	6½	7½	4½	2½	1½	—	—	4	2½	7½	4½
Cleobury N. Crossing	2 3	1 4	1 10	1 1	1 8	1 0	1 5	10	1 2	8½	10	6	5	3	4	2½	—	—	4	2½
Ditton Priors Halt ..	2 5	1 6	2 1	1 3	2 0	1 3	1 8	1 0	1 6	10½	1 2	8½	9	5½	7½	4½	4	2½	—	—

75 January 1st, 1928

Chance & Bland, Ltd., Printers Gloucester.

Above No. 29 attacks the 1 in 60 grade just outside Cleobury Junction on a Ditton Priors train in 1936.

S.H.P. Higgins

Below Cleobury Town station and yard in 1938. The ex-CM & DP offices are situated on the left, while on the right can be seen the offices of the Burwarton Coal and Trading Company and the weighbridge. Beyond these stands Cleobury Town engine shed, in front of which is the site of the sawmill. A mixed train for Ditton Priors is about to leave.

W.A. Camwel

0-6-0PT No. 2001. This locomotive was loaned to the Cleobury Mortimer & Ditton Priors Light Railway in 1914. It is standing outside the old Kidderminster shed.

A.G. Ellis

stock, anything larger being restricted from the branch. These coaches were now stabled at Cleobury Mortimer Junction usually on the small length of siding known as the "Monkey road".

From 1927 onwards it is interesting to see from an engine record book from Kidderminster shed some of the replacement engines that were sent to work the branch whilst Nos 28 and 29 were off duty. No. 28 was away in May 1927 and at this time a '2021' class 0-6-0PT, No 2101 was sent from Worcester shed, working the branch until 19th November, 1927 when it was returned to Worcester (WOS) having also deputized for No. 29, away for repairs.

In 1928 another engine was used as replacement. This time it was No. 1962 ('850' Class 0-6-0PT) in place of No. 28 away at Swindon. By 1928 the number of ex CM & DP open wagons in service was down to two. One, old No. 7, which had been given a heavy repair by the British Wagon Company after damage on the Light Railway, outlasted No. 8 by eight months. In 1928, too, the traffic from the Clee Hill Granite Company had ceased. The Magpie Quarry had problems with faulted rock and much uncommercial material was having to be dumped as waste, which, added to a general falling off in demand for dhustone, caused the bankruptcy of the Company. The Official Receiver ran the ropeway for a while to try to get some money back but the buckets finally came to a halt and the steel rope was sold as scrap for a substantial sum.

Mr Ernest Morris retired in this year having most successfully managed the Light Railway throughout its relatively short life. A most strict and correct man, according to those who knew him, but greatly respected by all who worked for him.

In charge of the Town station now was Porter/Station Master Mr Fred Harvey known to many as "Bozer" or "Bow". Naturally there were many different drivers and firemen from Kidderminster shed working on the branch now but Mr T. Dowding and Mr J. Howe were still regularly to be seen, Mr Howe living in one of the railway houses at Cleobury Town. Mr Bill Breakwell who began as a cleaner on the CM & DP was a fireman there at this period and Mr Fred Hills a driver from Kidderminster came to Cleobury Town shed. It was about this

time that Mr Ted Teague had been joined by Mr W. Futrill as guard and the branch gained its nickname amongst local railwaymen of "The Gadget". Although only 11 miles from Kidderminster the branch became a 'lodging' turn for the firemen sent from the parent shed but as it was virtually a 9 to 5 job most men would travel by a suitably early train from Kidderminster to Cleobury Junction and walk up the track to the Town shed to find the engine in steam lit up by the resident cleaner. Similarly at night after the train service had ended and the loco coaled, watered and locked away the men would return to the junction to catch the train home.

Another '850' class 0-6-0PT worked the branch in 1929 whilst No. 29 was at Worcester Factory and the same engine deputized again later in the year in place of No. 28. The engine concerned, No. 2019, finally went back to Worcester after failing with a 'hot box' at Cleobury Mortimer on 9th September, 1929. '2021' class 0-6-0PT No. 2051 was the next fresh engine on the branch arriving on 7th February, 1930 to stand in for No. 29 for a short period. Then on 1st September, 1930 0-6-0ST No. 28 *Cleobury* finally followed *Burwarton* to Swindon to be rebuilt as a pannier tank. On arrival there, she spent some time as a Swindon locomotive yard pilot before going into shops. No. 28 had previously been put to work in another capacity on one of her earlier visits to Swindon when she was diverted on the way at Gloucester to Lydney (LYD) shed to act as a stationary boiler whilst their usual one was out of service for three weeks. She had also been sent to Cheltenham for a month from 23rd March to 20th April, 1924.

A variety of locomotives was used on the branch whilst No. 28 was away for rebuilding, 0-6-0PT No. 2001 being dispatched from Worcester the day No. 28 went away. This locomotive was a most unpopular choice amongst crewmen in the cold weather for like its sister engine No. 2019 it was an '850' class still fitted with a half cab and only a storm sheet for protection when running back bunker first from Ditton Priors (locos always worked this way round from Light Railway days onwards).

It was exchanged for No. 2101 for a period of just over 2 months before Swindon sent 0-6-0T No. 803 (formerly *Ravelstone* of the Llanelly and Mynydd Mawr Railway). This

Above   The disused aerial ropeway discharge terminal at Detton Ford
on 30th March, 1938, looking towards Ditton Priors.

R.K. Cope

Below   Detton Ford platform in 1938, showing the concrete shelter and
concrete lamp standard with oil lamp.

R.K. Cope

engine failed in April 1931 when 0-6-0PT No. 1220 came as replacement from Worcester for a week. No. 803 was not a popular engine with the permanent way staff, being considered the cause of much extra track maintenance, and it was replaced from September 1931 by another absorbed 0-6-0T from South Wales. This locomotive had kept its original pre-grouping name of *Pioneer* and was now GWR No. 2187, once No. 8 of the Burry Port and Gwendraeth Valley Railway. This engine saw out the time of No. 28's absence and went back to Neath in February 1932, No. 28 having arrived back at Kidderminster in its rebuilt form the previous December.

When rebuilt Nos. 28 and 29 looked basically the same but there were superficial differences. On No. 28, the tank vents had been placed in a different position from No. 29, also on No. 28, handrails on the pannier tank side were not in line with those on the bunker, the cabside rail was continuous with the tankside, the footplate frame was not cut away at the cab steps, the beading on the bunker was different and the injectors showed some variation. Both Nos. 28 and 29 had whistle shields at some time in their lives. The rebuilt weight was given as 39 tons 18 cwt and under the GWR the locos were put into power class "A", yellow route.

Both engines lost their spacious cabs which caused complaints from the footplate staff and as a result a standard Great Western fireman's shovel was cut down in length to get a "good swing" into the firebox. Apart from this problem the locos proved just as reliable as they ever had been. From 1933 to 1936 there is no reference in the shed book to engines replacing branch locos which had gone away. Possibly traffic did not demand this cover now, and yet Cleobury Town yard was as busy as ever in this period of the thirties.

The Burwarton Coal and Trading Company, under the management of Mr W.E. Badger, now supplied a whole range of building materials to local merchants as well as coal, coke and lime. They had a delivery lorry driven by Mr Fred Teague (no relation to the GWR Guard) and in their office at Cleobury Town yard was Mr Herbert Higgins. Beyond the Burwarton

Company's depot but before the engine shed was Corbett's wood yard. Timber, mainly from the Boyne estate, was sawn up here under cover on large rack benches and made into wagon solebars, headstocks, and underframes. Rail chair keys were also cut and supplied to the GWR whilst some timber went for pit props. The machinery was driven by a steam engine operated by Mr Jess Stevens and in addition five other men worked inside on the saw benches whilst three worked outside including Mr W. Watkiss whose job it was, as a young boy, to stack the keys which were individually inspected by an official from the GWR. Mr Tom Carter, Mr A. Beeston and Mr Cliff Lloyd also worked here at this time. The whole organization was moved under the instructions of Mr A. Prattley, Corbett's engineer, to Lyonshall in 1935 or 1936 when the timber supply from the Burwarton estate fell away.

At Ditton Priors new rail-linked developments were still taking place in the early 1930s.

At this time, an asphalt plant was set up in Ditton Priors Yard, wagons of crushed stone arriving off the quarry in the Abdon Clee sidings behind the station. Stone was off loaded, lifted up to the top of the plant and covered in tar. Some was then taken by rail but more was carried away by road. In 1934 *Fleetwood* sustained damage to her cylinders and was not considered worth repairing, being left to rust at the terminus end of the Abdon Clee sidings in Ditton Priors yard. The Quarry Company eventually bought, in 1934, a Kerr, Stuart and Co Ltd 0-6-0T to replace the defunct *Fleetwood*. This was No. 3078 (built 1917) *Park*. It was sold again to R.R. Paton Ltd (Cardiff) in 1937.

In 1936 the last link with the CM & DP freight rolling stock was severed with the withdrawal of ex CM & DP Brake number 1. (GWR 10109) which had the distinction of being the longest serving goods vehicle from the Light Railway days. In 1938, the GWR finally decided that the passenger service had become uneconomic and it came as no great surprise to local residents when closure notices were displayed to take effect at the end of the summer services.

No. 29 on the 1 in 60 bank approaching Wyre Common Crossing with a short freight. Note the bogie wagon and crane used for loading timber.

S.H.P. Higgins

The two 0-6-0Ts tried on the CM & DP branch. *Above* 0-6-0T No. 2197 *Pioneer*, and *below* 0-6-0T
No. 803. Both locomotives were photographed at Llanelly on 28th August, 1938.

R.K. Cope

bove Prescott Siding, showing the simple corrugated iron goods shed, the oil
mp standard and the concrete facing to the platform. 30th March, 1938.
R.K. Cope

Below   Aston Botterell Siding looking towards Cleobury on the same day.
R.K. Cope

Cleobury Mortimer Junction, with No. 29 at the Ditton Priors branch platform in 1938. The branch closure notice is fixed to the Great Western pagoda shelter on the platform. The stock on the right is

No. 29 awaits the off at Ditton Priors, bound for Cleobury in 1938.

W.A. Camwell

Left View of the Ditton Priors line curve out of Cleobury Mortimer Junction in May 1938. The signals control access to the GWR station.

R.K. Cope

Right Wyre Crossing at the summit of the 1 in 60 gradient between Cleobury Town and Cleobury Junction. Note the cattle guards and immaculate permanent way. 11th May, 1938.

R.K. Cope

Left Stop board at Wyre Crossing where Cleobury Junction bound freight trains stopped to pin down brakes.

R.K. Cope

Below Level crossing gates at Cleobury Town. Gate nearest the camera is of RNAD pattern, while that in the background is a Great Western type. 4th June, 1965.

R.S. Carpenter

Bottom No. 29 at Cleobury Town with Fireman Bill Breakwell on engine, Driver J. Howe and Guard W. Futrill by engine, Guard Ted Teague on extreme left.

Authors' Collection, per N. Howe

Above Driver J. Howe, who lived at Cleobury Town, off to get his supper. The line of private owner wagons includes a Burwarton Coal Co. vehicle.

Authors' Collection, per N. Howe

Below Driver Jim Howe and Fireman Bill Breakwell pose on ex-LMM 0-6-0T No. 803 on its visit to the CM & DP in 1931.

Authors' Collection, per N. Howe

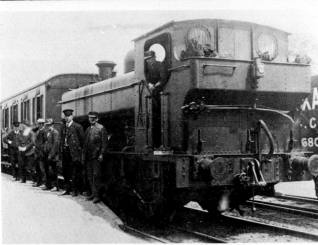

Above Line of private owner wagons at Cleobury Town on 30th March, 1938.
R.K. Cope

Below No. 29 outside Cleobury Town shed (by now, a sub-shed to Kidd-
minster) in 1938.
W.A. Camw

Left Level crossing at Cleobury Town, looking towards Ditton Priors on 4th June, 1965.

R.K. Cope

Right Chilton Siding and remains of the private platform (on right), seen on 30th March, 1938.

R.K. Cope

Below The concrete shelter, cattle grid and GWR rail stop blocks feature in this view of Detton Ford. The line to the ropeway sidings is just visible on the right.

A. Muckley

Left The level crossing at Prescott, seen from the south on 24th September, 1938.

R.K. Co[...]

Left No. 29 leaves Stottesdon for Cleobury in 193[...] The little used siding road is in the foreground.

S.H.P. Higg[...]

Below Stottesdon Halt on 30th March, 1938, whic[...] possessed a standard design CM & DP wood[...] waiting shelter.

R.K. Co[...]

bove Burwarton station, with No. 28 on a Ditton Priors train. The platform cings are of local Abdon Clee concrete. The platform height was raised in WR days.

W.A. Camwell

Below No. 29 shunting at Burwarton.

Authors' Collection, per N. Howe

Above A mixed train at Ditton Priors terminus, headed by No. 28. An ex-CM &
DP brake van is still in use at the end of the train. The Abdon Clee Quarry
Company's sidings pass behind the station buildings on the right.

P. Robinson/Lens of Sutton

Below   Cleobury North platform and gated crossing on 30th March, 1938. T
milk churn type containers were used for transporting young trout from Lo
Boyne's hatcheries at nearby Mill Farm.

R.K. Co

ve Ditton Priors terminus in the mid-Thirties, with the tarmac plant and
ading gantry visible behind the station platform. Note the platform exten-
and the concrete works in the distance.

Authors' Collection

Below Shunting at Ditton Priors. The vehicle next to No. 29 is brake van No.
68873 which arrived new in 1936 to replace one of the CM & DP brake vans.
Behind the locomotive is the engine house of the tarmac plant.

R.K. Cope

SPECIAL NOTICE

DISCONTINUANCE OF
PASSENGER TRAIN SERVICE

BETWEEN

CLEOBURY MORTIMER

AND

DITTON PRIORS

The Great Western Railway give notice that on and from MONDAY, SEPTEMBER 26th, 1938, the Passenger Train service on the above Line will be withdrawn and the following trains cancelled :—

9.30 a.m. Cleobury Mortimer to Ditton Priors.
2.24 p.m. (Wednesdays only) Cleobury Mortimer to Ditton Priors.
5.20 p.m. Cleobury Mortimer to Ditton Priors.
11.10 a.m. Ditton Priors to Cleobury Mortimer.
3.50 p.m. (Wednesdays only) Ditton Priors to Cleobury Mortimer.
6.23 p.m. Ditton Priors to Cleobury Mortimer.

The Platforms at the undermentioned places will be closed to Passengers :—

CLEOBURY TOWN HALT   ASTON BOTTERELL SIDING
DETTON FORD SIDING   BURWARTON HALT
PRESCOTT SIDING   CLEOBURY NORTH CROSSING
STOTTESDON HALT   DITTON PRIORS HALT

The Company will continue to run one Goods train in each direction over the Line on week-days only, and so afford facilities for the conveyance of Parcels traffic, Minerals, Livestock and General Merchandise to and from the above-mentioned places.

Particulars of the arrangements may be obtained on application to the Station Master, Cleobury Mortimer, Mr. J. E. POTTER, Divisional Superintendent, Worcester (Shrub Hill Station) (Telephone 1530), or Mr. J. A. WARREN-KING, District Goods Manager, Worcester (Shrub Hill Station) (Telephone 1530).

PADDINGTON STATION,
July, 1938.   JAMES MILNE,
                                               General Manager.

Notice announcing the withdrawal of passenger services on the Ditton Priors branch from 26th September, 1938.

G.F. Bannister

The last passenger train was run with great enthusiast interest on Saturday 24th September, 1938, there being no Sunday service. The final train on that Saturday was to be the 5.20 pm from Cleobury Mortimer. In spite of protests and petitions from local residents for the service to be kept on, the threats of closure made before by the GWR were now to be carried out. The local staff were surprised by the affectionate interest that the line engendered from people outside the vicinity and the seventy odd mourners who arrived to ride the last train had to be swiftly provided for by two extra four wheeled vehicles added to the normal brake third and composite pair. Nothing larger was permitted by the Rule Book, 6 wheel and bogie coaches being banned although bogie stock such as those vehicles coded by the GWR as 'Snakes' B and C, 'Siphons' G and H and 'Monsters' were allowed.

The Guard on duty that day, Mr Frederick Somers, could not move his train out until 5.48 pm, amidst cheers from the visitors but according to the *Kidderminster Times*, their mood was not echoed by locals standing alongside the line in the fine Autumn drizzle. The train engine No. 28 (No. 29 being away under repair) pulled out of Ditton Priors for the return journey on what should have been the 6.23 pm with Mr J. Clutterbuck at the regulator and an impossible 33 minutes to make up in order to keep time for the connection at Cleobury Mortimer. The gas supply in the carriages had run out so the last part of the historic return journey was made without carriage lights. Fireworks lit at Cleobury Mortimer on the arrival of the branch train showed up the waiting coaches of the Kidderminster train which had been held back to make the connection.

Following the last rites of the passenger service the GWR provided only a daily afternoon goods train worked by a locomotive which ran light to and from Kidderminster to perform the duty, Cleobury Town shed having already closed in July 1938.

Industry at Ditton Priors was in decline, the quarrying operations had been transferred to an area away from the inclined railway although the concrete works and asphalt plant were still in business. The locomotives *Trent* and *Kingswood* had earlier been cut up on top of the Hill and brought down in wagons loaded as scrap, whilst *Fleetwood* was dealt with where it had been stranded for years rusting away amongst the undergrowth.

Of the last three footplatemen from former Light Railway days, Driver T. Dowding retired, whilst Driver J. Howe and Fireman Bill Breakwell were transferred to Kidderminster along with (ex-KDR) Driver J. Clutterbuck. The Stationmaster at Cleobury Town, Mr Fred Harvey was no longer needed there and eventually transferred to the station staff at Cleobury Mortimer.

The future for "The Gadget" in the Autumn of 1938 looked very bleak indeed but the turn of international events changed the picture entirely.

Above In fine autumn drizzle, No. 28 has arrived at the Ditton Priors terminus with the last passenger train from Cleobury on 24th September, 1938. The tarmac plant and engine house are behind the water column.

R.K. Cope

Below No. 28 couples up to its train for the last passenger run to Cleobury Junction on the same day.

R.K. Cope

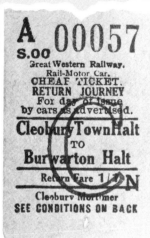

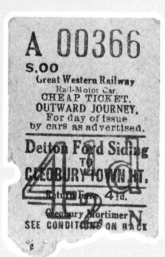

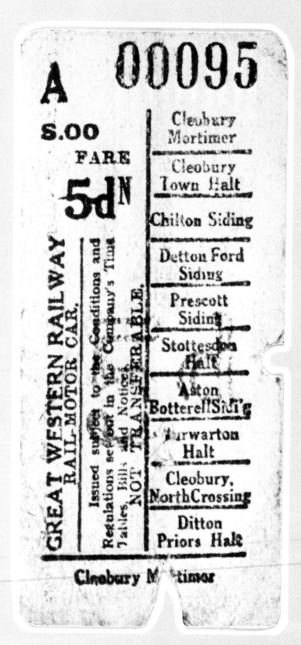

Above   An example of the later style of Great Western card ticket.

G.F. Bannister

Left   Three examples of early Great Western Williamson paper tickets used on the branch.

Authors' Collection, per Mrs. F. Harvey

CHAPTER NINE

Working the Abdon Quarry Railways

THE fortunes of the CM & DP and the Abdon Clee Quarry Company were inextricably linked and so, following absorption by the GWR, were those of the branch line and the quarry railway which remained under independent existence.

The day's work in the quarry just before the First World War started at 6 am which could mean setting off to walk to work from surrounding villages as early as 4 am for there was the daunting ¾ hour walk up to the top of the hill before a further stiff climb to the actual quarry face unless one was lucky and worked in the crushing plant area. In the period before 1914 much of the stone was used for tramways and was patiently chipped and hewn into 6″ x 9″ setts by the sett makers using only primitive hand tools and usually working in the open air.

At this time stone was also crushed and screened into various sizes in the Abdon Quarry itself and in addition to the buildings involved in these operations there was a blacksmith's shop, carpenter's shop, fitter's shop and a small wooden loco shed to house one of the quarry's standard gauge locomotives. There were also small cottages close by the quarry area lived in by quarry workers notably the quarry's own horseman with his charges in stables close by. A small concrete making plant is known to have existed even before the First World War and may well have been responsible for turning out the concrete drainage pipes used in the construction of the Light Railway.

Following the return of men from the war the working day was cut from 10 hours to 8 hours with a 7 am start and a "piece work" payment system. The three ex W.D. Motor Railway vehicles arrived for the quarry company to replace the sole 2ft gauge steam loco of which little is known.

After the war Mr James Ritchie, a Scot like Mr Hamish Cross, was in overall charge as Quarry foreman with Doug Morris as his assistant. Charlie Cooper was foreman over the crushers with Jack Cleeton the crusher feeder, tipping the stone to be crushed from narrow gauge wagons. The crusher's machinery was driven by a large gas engine looked after by Bill Hodnet, the gas being produced from anthracite in a building known as the "gas plant".

Up until 1918 horses were used to haul the stone. The wagons were pulled from the different quarry faces where men were employed breaking stone and loading it into the wagons. In charge of the horses was Job James, assisted by Will Mountain and Bert Cartwright. Old Job was quite a hand with comb and scissors and when not attending his horses was kept busy cutting hair using an upturned bucket as his barber's chair, presumably the "Gaffer" turned a blind eye to these occasions. With the coming of the Motor Rail vehicles in 1918, the horses were relegated to hauling only the empty wagons up to the faces but stood in when the inevitable breakdown of the ex W.D. machines occurred. The new vehicles were usually driven by Charlie Harris, Horace Hodnett and Harold Bradley, a small post and panel shed having been provided to house them. Harold Bradley who started work in 1921 for 24/-(£1.20p) per week in the concrete works then flourishing in Ditton Priors yard, recalls how the "whizz-bangs" as they became known could pull 16 loaded wagons, about 30 tons from the quarry faces to the top of the inclines leading down to the crushing

plant. The uncoupled wagons would be let run down by gravity towards an unloading gantry at the rear of the crushing plant, where a spragger was employed to brake the wagons on their downward run by thrusting a stout wooden billet into the wheels. A loaded wagon would stand permanently on the downslope side of the spragger, often Mr Richard Handley, as a buffer stop in case he missed his wheel. There was one fatality from a runaway however when Mr Wilf Morris was sadly struck down pushing an empty back up the incline, his view obscured of a full wagon hurtling down towards him and despite warning shouts he died from injuries received in the accident. This was one of the very few serious accidents known to have occurred on the quarry railways over a period of 30 years.

Derailments on the roughly laid narrow gauge track were few and far between, those that did occur could be put down to driver error, like one made by Charlie Harris in a rush to get away for a visit to the annual Shrewsbury Flower Show. He came around a curve too quickly and turned over his "whizz-bang" pulling over the following loaded wagons. Needless to say, having to clear up the mess on his own he did not get to the flower show that year!

The stone, when crushed and screened, would be discharged through hoppers into standard gauge wagons waiting below. The loco *Trent* first loaned to the Quarry by Bott and Stennett was driven by George Fullaway, himself a Bott and Stennett man. Later Artie Hall became the driver with Will Mountain's son Jack as his "rope runner". The "rope-runners" job was basically that of shunter coupling and uncoupling the wagons between the plant and the top of the incline.

From the three discharging terminals the loaded wagons would be taken to the top of the incline having passed over a weighbridge on the way. On arrival at the top of the incline, the wagons would be marshalled into twos and threes and taken onto a concrete platform in front of the rope's drum, the cable from which ran underground at this point and came out from a pit just near the top of the incline. The cable was coupled up to an empty wagon called a "dummy". The loco then gently pushed the wagons over the top of the incline till all the weight was taken up by the rope acting on the drum.

After telephoning the yard at Ditton Priors to get the all clear, the brakesman would gently let the wagons down at a moderate pace, the empty ones being brought up in the self acting process passing the loaded vehicles on a turnout.

The first brakesman was Bert Hall brother of Artie Hall the loco driver, followed afterwards by Cyril Bradshaw. They had the responsible task of keeping the wagons under control and not over running on the incline. Originally some form of coloured indicators and bells were in use to tell them when the wagons were at journey's end, as a visual look out of the brake house windows was no guarantee of seeing the wagons, especially when the heavy mists, common on the hill, obscured the view. Extra vigil was certainly needed later when the indicator no longer functioned, with only a piece of cloth or large handkerchief tied to the rope as a guide. It must have been quite an experience to see wagons loom out of the fog!

Down the incline at the turnout Fred Cawdrey and Jim Cartwright were employed to keep the points well greased and generally make sure the rope stayed under the roller guides to prevent the rope breaking, thereby causing a runaway. Only two runaways occurred on the incline, the first on the trial runs, the other much later in the nineteen thirties. The latter was attributed to the hot weather at the time, the rails buckling causing a partial derailment and breaking the rope in the process. However, it is suggested that the rope then in use was of a smaller diameter than the original and could have parted through overstrain.

Mr Cross was very quick to get a replacement rope, Charlie Cooper and other men virtually working day and night to reconnect it, and as a safeguard against further breakages a spare rope was obtained and laid down one side of the incline. The damage on both occasions was to quarry property only, the wagons being scattered in various bits and pieces over the fields adjoining the turnout.

The incline was in fact the quarry's lifeline, for as well as the stone, hay for the horses, petrol for the "whizz-bangs" and for some years even the men's wages were all carried in the wagons.

Mr Ben Bowen relates how as a youngster he used to stand on the bridge at Oakwood eagerly awaiting the descent of the wagons and how the rope guide rollers under the bridge would continue to revolve long after the wagons had passed. Down in the yard at Ditton were two standard gauge locos *Kingswood* and *Fleetwood*, their job being to shuttle loaded and empty wagons between the bottom of the incline at Oakwood and Ditton Priors yard.

The driver of these engines for many years was Will Rigby, with Archie Cartwright as his "rope runner" and as well as being busy marshalling wagons for the Light Railway, wagons of fine dhustone and cement for the concrete works set up in the yard where shunted. When not in use one loco was kept in a small wooden engine shed behind the station platform, the other being stabled outside in the open, the shed not being big enough for both.

In setting up the concrete works in the 1914/1918 war, Mr Hamish Cross must have been a man of vision, for reinforced concrete was in its infancy at the time and was of an unknown quantity. His idea in setting up the plant was to make prefabricated buildings using a standard 'post and panel' principle, all parts sliding or fitting together so easily that unskilled labour could be used for assembly thus cutting down costs. The concrete was made in a large shed from a mixture of

cement and dhustone chippings being poured into wooden moulds (seen in photo) and left to harden off, after which the moulds would be lifted off to be used again, the finished article being left to weather and stockpiled in the yard. In the concrete works yard was a narrow gauge track used for transporting the concrete parts on 4 wheeled bogies hauled by a "whizz-bang" out of the mixing area in the shed. A dead end siding ran alongside a wharf where with the aid of a crane the materials could be loaded onto wagons for transportation to all parts of the country.

The plant proved a valuable asset to the quarry company in supplying the buildings mentioned elsewhere as well as some half a dozen houses known as the "smallholdings" built in Ditton Priors ostensibly for ex service men from the 1914/18 war.

Another innovation which had taken place on the hill top in the years prior to the First World War was a small tarmac plant set up as an experiment, using fine dhustone mixed with tar. The plant was rather a crude affair; tar placed on iron plates was heated from underneath using coal from the long disused pits on the hill and when in a fluid state, men wearing clogs because of the heat would scatter the stone over it. When cool the resultant mixture was then manhandled into wagons and sent down the incline to be used on the roads. It proved a great success and the Abdon Co. was soon advertising this tarmac as "Asphalt Carpet" in their catalogue.

The advancement of the petrol engine in the nineteen twenties meant an ever increasing demand for improved roads, and with the population moving out to the urban areas of large cities problems of housing were created. During this period of the twenties the Abdon Quarry Co. provided employment when the area, and indeed the country as a whole, was in a depressed state. Orders for houses and other buildings and road material meant extra men being taken on as well as extra plant to cope with the demand. The quarry work force had risen to over two hundred, local men being joined by casual workers from outside the area. The Abdon Co. built two rows of houses in Hall Farm Road, Ditton Priors for some of its employees, but the "casuals" were not so lucky. They had to be content with a night's lodging or, as was often the case, sleeping rough in any convenient out-building. Many of these men were known by an alias usually taken from the area they came from, for example "Broseley Billy" "Pontesbury Tommy" and one named "Pincher Joe". They worked alongside the regular work force amongst whom

Abdon Clee Stone Quarry works with crushing machinery in the background. The shuttering on the cab of 0-6-0ST *Trent* was provided as a draught excluder. A rake of narrow gauge tipper wagons stands to the right of *Trent*.   *Authors' Collection*

Above Inclined railway looking down towards Ditton Priors before the CM & DP had reached the terminus there. The three-rail track was used as far as the turnout where it merged into single track as far as the wagon exchange loop at Oakwood.

W. Atkinson

Below A view looking up the incline during its construction in 1907.

W. Atkinson

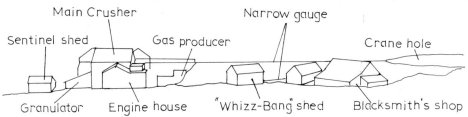

Above Abdon Quarry, showing the various buildings and narrow gauge lines serving the area.
Authors' Collection

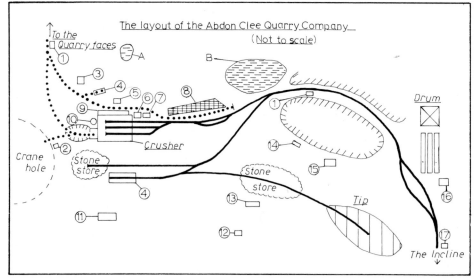

KEY

1 — Weighbridge
2 — Diesel winch
3 — Blacksmith
4 — Engine shed
5 — Fitters
6 — Granulator
7 — Sentinel
8 — Sett making area
9 — Engine house
10 — Gas producer
11 — Stables
12 — Powder magazine
13 — Stone washer
14 — Tar mixer
15 — Concrete works
16 — Brake House
17 — Office

•••• Narrow gauge

——— Standard gauge

Reservoirs
A-For Sentinel
B-For Locos

Left Plan of the Abdon Quarry complex.

Right Rope drum at the top of the incline.
The hut on the right is the brake house.
Authors' Collection

Left Wagons arriving at the top of the incline,
passing over the trough for the rope.
Authors' Collection

Right Loaded wagons descending the incline, with a "dummy" at the front.
Authors' Collection

were Fred Wright, Max Cartwright, Clem Cartwright, Harry Parker, George, Alf and Wilf Morris, Len Oxley, Harry Hall, Sid Proctor, Bob Jackson, George Dyke, Charlie Locke, Jack Morris and Jack Oxley. Jack Oxley was foreman platelayer responsible for all the railway track in the quarry, whilst Reg Green was the explosives man, Cliff Bowen when not working in the faces also helped out as "rope runner". Alec Norman the blacksmith and his striker Bill Pearce were kept busy shoeing the horses and making and sharpening sett makers tools. Tom Eames was foreman fitter over Will Scandrett and Alec Ritchie, the "Gaffer's" son, who were kept busy repairing the machinery or looking after the locos.

In the middle twenties the demand for setts was slowly falling off and what setts were required began to be cut by machine rather than the laborious hand method. Conditions of work in the quarry although improved by this kind of machinery were still harsh. At this time the crushing plant was not covered in, exposing the men who worked there to the biting winds of the hill top and covering them and everything else with a fine coating of dust. If the weather was very bad work stopped and so did the wages! The men sheltered in the warm surroundings of the gas plant at such times until the weather improved enough for work to begin again. Wages, however, were comparatively good when contrasted to that of the farm labourer on the estates below the hill. It was not unknown, at the time, for a quarry man to earn £5 a week on piece work compared to 25/- (£1.25p) for the farm labourer. In the "Howard Arms", Ditton Priors the casuals would gather on most evenings to wash the dust out of their throats, shirt sleeved, sporting old battered hats and in "bracers" but most distinctively wearing the gaiter-like garment of cloth worn by all quarry men and known as "yocks". Tucked down their trouser leg they usually kept a large stick known as

"the old man" used for scraping dirt off picks, shovels and other tools. In this guise they often entertained the pub regulars with a dance or jig. At closing time they bid everybody goodnight and set off in search for the cosiest place to sleep the night. They were well liked in the village and it was with great sorrow that the news came of a "casual" frozen to death sleeping under a hedge or for example of "Pincher Joe" found drowned in a pool at Oakwood.

Whilst the demand for setts fell the need for track ballast increased during the nineteen twenties and on occasions GWR 20 ton hoppers were sent up the incline. The Quarry Co. had large stockpiles of 1½" grade stone for which there had previously been no sale but a new order from the GWR meant they could profitably dispose of it, although from the quarry workers point of view very tediously. Armed with a small rake, "loaders-up" would rake stone into a steel basket, fashioned in the blacksmiths shop and with this strapped to their bodies, they would then have to climb a ladder and deposit the stone into the hoppers, two men on piece rate taking a whole day to load 20 tons of stone!

At this time also *Trent* had been joined on the top by *Kingswood* which had deputized whilst its sister was away being repaired following the fire in the engine shed.

Thereafter both engines remained on top owing to the difficulty of getting them up and down the incline, one engine working, the other as spare, although it was not unknown, if absolutely necessary, for either one of them to be sent down to help out *Fleetwood* in the yard.

The livery of *Fleetwood* and *Kingswood* was maroon with black and gold lining, that of *Trent* being all green.

The continued development of modern tarred road making methods meant setting up extra plant and machinery both on

Hudswell, Clarke 0-6-0ST No. 313 *Fleetwood*, out of use at the old tar plant at the Cleobury end of Ditton Yard.   *F. Jones*

Fleetwood decaying at the top end of Ditton yard, still displaying traces of lining out.
P.W. Robinson/Lens of Sutton

the hill and below in Ditton Priors. On the hill near the crushers, a machine called a granulator was set up. It was powered by a stationary Sentinel engine driven by Stan Painter and received stone that had been previously crushed, but was now ground down in the machine to form "chippings". These chippings were then either used in the tarmac plant on the hill or sent down in trucks to a similar plant in Ditton, but after some years this proved uneconomical and in 1933 a larger tarmac plant was built by the Abdon Quarry Co's own staff. Alec Ritchie and Kaleb Blomberg, a Russian who had previously been a ship's carpenter, were mainly responsible for the erection of the steel work, Kaleb benefiting from his sea going experience in the rigging of sailing ships getting the girders and cross pieces up without trouble. The plant was virtually self contained, stone chippings were off loaded from the trucks, usually by George Morris and Harry Hall onto a "Zimmer" conveyor which took the stone into the bottom of the plant. The stone was then preheated and put into a bucket elevator, hoisting the stone to the top of the plant. Here it was weighed on a small weighbridge, then a measured amount of liquid was poured over it in a skip. The skip was then trundled out onto a gantry over the railway tracks to be emptied below to waiting trucks or lorries. The lorry-borne asphalt always had to be away early to get to its site before road traffic built up meaning usually a 6 am start for the men in the plant. The buckets and conveyor machinery was driven by a stationary "Ruston" engine which also supplied steam to heating coils in a large underground concrete tank containing liquid bitumen to keep it fluid, regular deliveries being brought by road by Shell-Mex.

The lorry traffic both for stone and asphalt was preferred to rail borne traffic especially by local councils as it could be delivered "on site" cutting down time wasted unloading railway wagons to road vehicles. Stone had, in previous years, been conveyed by road, first by Sentinel or Foster steam wagons owned by the Quarry Co, but local hauliers, amongst them Southerns, Frank Jones, and Galbraiths of Wolverhampton were more often employed in the early 1930's in preference to the GWR and even then the quarry supply situation was changing.

On Abdon the dhustone cap had all gone by now so the Quarry Co were forced to burrow down into the rock surface for new supplies and a large crater was opened up. This area was known as the "Crane Hole" because of the large cranes equipped with a skip to bring the stone out (see diagram on page 78). When the hole was too deep for the crane to reach the stone, narrow gauge lines were laid down a steep gradient into the hole, and being too steep for "whizz-bang" haulage a Gardner diesel powered winch was installed to bring the tippers out, these being clipped to the wire rope and hauled out. Harold Bradley was transferred from the "whizz-bangs" to look after the winch, earning an extra 2d per day in the process. His place on the "whizz-bangs" was taken by Dick Glaze and Arthur Caines.

A lot of unwanted rubbish was taken from the hole, and with the natural waste from the quarries a sizeable tip built up making an extra task for *Trent* or *Kingswood* shuttling back and forth with the spoil. Meanwhile, down in Ditton Priors yard, further trouble beset the Company when in 1934 *Fleetwood* now being driven by Archie Cartwright sustained damage to her cylinders and on inspection the repair costs were considered too great, the engine being all but life expired anyway.

Above Manning, Wardle 0-6-0ST No. 729 *Kingswood* shunting at Ditton Priors. The stovepipe chimney was fashioned in the blacksmith's shop on the hill after the original had burnt away.

P.W. Robinson/Lens of Sutton

Below Kingswood outside her shed at Ditton Priors. Rope runner Jack Mountain and Driver Archie Cartwright are on the locomotive. *F. Jones*

Kerr Stuart 0-6-0T No. 3078 *Park* at Newlands, NCB.

F. Jones

Kerr-Stuart *Park* in green livery was hastily acquired to fill the gap, arriving by rail a few days after *Fleetwood* had been condemned. It was soon put to work shunting the concrete and tarmac plants and the traffic from the incline, but it was considered too heavy and unsuitable for this duty by Archie Cartwright, and because of its small steam space usually primed up the grade to Oakwood. Archie remembers being a little sad when *Fleetwood* was shunted up to the end of the yard and left for the vegetation to grow up around her.

It was plain, early in 1936, that the days of the Abdon Quarries were numbered, only two mixed trains a day now ran on the GWR, a sign of the rapidly diminishing stone supply, road transport having what little trade there was. The Quarry Co. looking for other stone deposits obtained a lease on land over the hill at Cockshutt and decided to switch operations there when stone was found. There was talk of running an aerial ropeway over the hill to connect this new quarry to the incline but the idea soon foundered when costs were worked out.

The plant at Abdon was allowed to run down and by the end of June had closed altogether. Some men and machinery were transferred to Cockshutt including one "whizz-bang", Mr Will Cartwright being sent as driver. Being only a small quarry with a limited potential output only a small crushing plant was set up driven by a Crossley Diesel engine and consequently the work force was small and very versatile. Alec Ritchie or sometimes Harry Parker had the job of driving the Bedford lorry carrying about 20 workmen to and from Cockshutt from Ditton each day then hauling stone around the area all day, having to find time also to grease and service the lorry!

The men not wanted in this quarry either took jobs locally or were re-employed in the tarmac or concrete works both still having valuable contracts, the latter having orders for a new product namely concrete roadside kerbs with reflective glass set in them. There had also been some experiment with insulating material for the cavity spaces in the Abdon building and two other forward looking ideas are worthy of note. For some time Mr Cross had been trying to make an early form of "cats eye" using a 4″ x 1″ block of concrete stuck to which was a rubber pad with glass set in. This project and another in which concrete was laid on rubber to make a quiet resilient road together with the insulatory material only failed to be successful for want of suitable adhesives at the time.

During the early part of 1937 the Sheffield firm of Simms-Lewis (Dismantlers) moved into the area to cut up equipment left on the hill. As well as bringing their own staff they recruited men locally to help with the task and amongst the team were ex-quarry men Will Mountain, Will Scandrett, Jack Morris, the Handleys, father and son together with Edwin Cartwright and Ben Bowen both about 17 or 18 at the time. Although neither of these men had worked in the quarries, they had in fact worked for the Quarry Co. doing odd work here and there, Ben actually leaving school to work for Hamish Cross at "Oldfield", Ditton Priors as a kind of houseboy for 10/- (50p) per week, followed by a short time of employment in the concrete works under foreman-carpenter Will Wroe.

Up on the top of Abdon a good deal of equipment was cut up with oxy-acetylene torches, but some was broken with sledge hammers, as Edwin Cartwright can testify, wagers being lost or won on who could break the most during a day's work. Ben Bowen can remember struggling up the hill with a full gas cylinder over his shoulder, but not he adds without a few stops. Everything was cut up, and sorted into ferrous and non ferrous piles, even *Trent* and *Kingswood* suffered the same indignity of being cut into manageable parts and sent down the incline in the trucks, as were, it is believed, two of the "whizz-bangs".

The incline finally closed after the passage of the last trucks of scrap and a start was made lifting the track and dismantling the huge drum, a local farmer from Hillside even helping out with his tractor.

Explosives were used on the drum to try and blow the bearings off the shaft but made no impression, so it had to be cut up piece by piece. Whilst this was in progress Ben Bowen remembers, when working in a mist on the morning of 30th June 1937, a low flying aircraft was heard close by; it passed over the hill only to crash a few minutes later at Stanton Long, the occupants, all R.A.F. men being killed.

All the track was manhandled onto bogies, taken to the yard and processed. Even the rope was cut up, *Park* being employed at Oakwood drawing the rope with the aid of shackles, a length at a time down the hill, this being cut up with the aid of the torches. This was to be her last job for *Park* was no longer needed and was sent away to R.R. Paton Ltd Cardiff by November 1937, her driver Archie Cartwright being transferred to the concrete works.

Simms-Lewis's main gang including Ben Bowen were transferred to the Titterstone Quarries near Ludlow to cut up equipment there leaving behind a small work force and sub contractors Thomas Ward & Co. Ltd. and Eli Pearson & Co. both of Sheffield to cut up several Abdon wagons left in the yard. *Fleetwood* was cut up by Eli Pearson before the end of 1937, for by then all the sub-contractors had left.

The Abdon Quarries last big order was for stone being used during the winter of 1938/39 on a new by-pass at Church Stretton and although the concrete and tarmac works were still in operation a warning note was sounded in an article in the *Bridgnorth Journal* for 25th March, 1939. Figures released locally showed over 250 men unemployed in the quarries in the Ludlow district alone, although some men had been persuaded to give up their traditional craft and work on a new R.A.F. maintenance unit at Hartlebury, near Kidderminster whilst others with men from Ditton had been given temporary employment on the Church Stretton by-pass.

From the closing of the incline stone had been brought from the Cockshutt quarries by road in Frank Jones's Commer lorries regularly driven by Jack Lewis. At the asphalt plant where railway trucks had once been, these lorries stood on the overgrown tracks under the loading gantry to receive the loads of asphalt but this was not to last much longer. Later in 1939 the Cockshutt dhustone quarry was worked out, operations then being moved down the hill to the hamlet of Cockshuttford,

where deposits of the softer limestone had been found. This stone although suitable for roadmaking was too soft for concrete; the Quarry Co, after their stockpiles had gone was forced to buy in dhustone from Titterstone Quarries to keep the concrete works going. The war clouds broke in Sept 1939 bringing more labour problems as many of the younger men either volunteered or would eventually be called up. However, the concrete plant was still busy when war broke out, making concrete road blocks, land mines and kerb stones for the intended Naval armament depot, and to fill gaps being left by some of the young men, women were employed. Mrs May Childs (May Blount at the time) with her sister Elsie, Lettie Mountain, Mabel Cartwright and Bertha Green all worked alongside the men mixing the concrete or on other tasks. Some of the men employed were: — George Morris, Fred Morris, Ben Evans, Sid Proxton and of course Archie Cartwright. The tar plant latterly manned by Sid James, Harry Morris and his father were still in business but not for long after the outbreak of war.

When Messrs Bryants completed building the R.N.A. Depot at Ditton Priors in 1941, first the concrete plant shut down, quickly followed in 1942 by the tar plant. The Depot had come at a crucial time for the older men who although too old for army service still had years to give, and many took jobs within the Depot. Many had given 30 years service to Abdon Quarry and now went on to give the rest of their working life, in most cases another twenty or so years to the Depot.

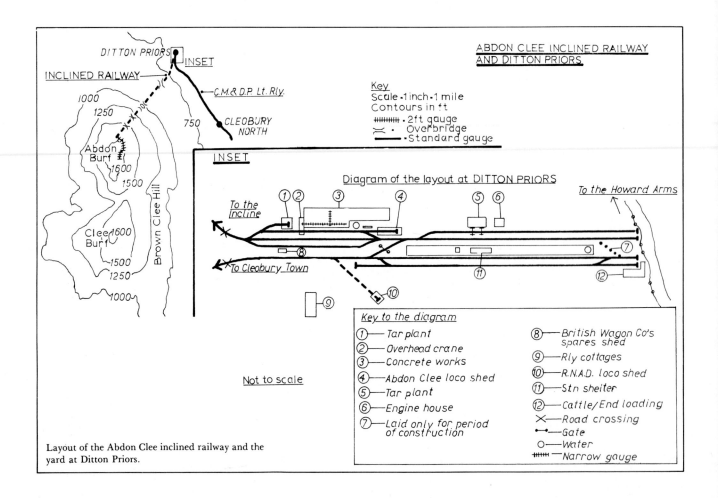

Layout of the Abdon Clee inclined railway and the yard at Ditton Priors.

CHAPTER TEN

The Second World War and BR Days

EVEN before the start of the Second World War, Britain's armament production had increased to such proportions as a result of the 1938 Munich crisis that areas for the storage of ammunition had to be sought. The ideal site would be somewhere isolated yet not without transport facilities.

The CM & DP branch and especially the Ditton Priors terminus area fitted these requirements completely and so was subsequently chosen by the Admiralty for the establishment of a Naval armament depot. Shortly after the passenger service had ceased "Nissen" huts were to be seen unobtrusively placed at outlying places in readiness for dumps that were also to be established at stations up the line and it is interesting to wonder here how much influence world events had on the ending of the passenger services! However, the choice having been made, a new lease of life was ensured for the branch.

Following the start of the hostilities in 1939 the commercial freight service was suspended from September 11th and No. 29 was sent to Worcester Works to have a spark arresting cowl fitted to her chimney in order, initially, to protect vans loaded with ammunition from stray sparks thrown out when the loco was working hard up the grades on the branch and later for working into the armament depot itself. In this guise No. 29 worked the branch daily taking ammunition to the dumps from trains at Cleobury Junction plus the odd wagon of coal for Chilton siding, or ballast for the railway's everyday maintenance needs, until mid 1941 when the R.N.A. Depot at Ditton Priors, being built by Bryants (Builders) of Birmingham was nearing completion. The depot was situated just to the east of Ditton Priors village, on land made available by Lord Boyne, although some railway land was taken up also, part of the old CM & DP line actually running through the depot!

To enable the depot to be filled quickly an old friend of the line 0-6-0PT No. 2001 was summoned from Worcester in July 1941, duly fitted with a cowl, and with 29 and 28 ran double headed trains with loads far exceeding the normal peacetime limits.

Such was the urgency that to save the locos running back light to Kidderminster shed for coaling, they would be stabled each day at Cleobury Junction with a supply of loco coal, stored in wagons, the engine crews having to do their coaling by hand.

Also stabled at the junction, on the back road behind the booking office, were three clerestory coaches, which, in more peaceful times did duty as camping coaches but now acted as accommodation for the naval reservists and marines sent to guard the ammunition trains. Similarly other old GWR coaches were placed at strategic points along the branch for use by other security personnel.

Whilst the armament depot was being established, GWR locos were allowed to work right through to Ditton Priors terminus, with security staff riding on the train, the crewmen having to surrender matches, cigarettes etc, which were then locked in a "contraband" box in the guard's van. Eventually the area was completely surrounded by a security fence and became a blank space on revised Ordnance Survey maps.

After the enclosure of the site, trains would stop at the perimeter fence, the engine "whistling up" for a gate to be opened, before proceeding with the security staff to one of the two transfer sheds, which had been built over loops known as

the explosives area.

At this point a small "Planet" diesel mechanical shunter (which had arrived in 1941 being hauled from Cleobury Junction to Ditton by No. 2001) would take over the marshalling of the wagons. The GWR loco could, if water was required, then run forward to replenish its tanks from the column at the terminus passing out of the other end of the depot through another gate in the fence.

The need for water posed a problem for the GWR operating staff, for a lot of shunting was carried out at the outlying dumps, often leaving the locos very short, so short sometimes that it was doubtful if they could have run to the columns either at Cleobury Town or Ditton Priors. This problem however was promptly solved by the Admiralty staff who, when required, would send a fire tender by road to the loco at the required place or if this was not available, an auxiliary pump could be sent instead, the loco then being watered from one of the many streams that ran beside the line.

As the war progressed, searchlight batteries were set up at several places along the line, including Goesland, as well as fire decoys on the nearby Clee Hills, as the depot had become of strategic importance enough even to get a mention on the German wartime programme broadcast by "Lord Haw Haw". However, apart from a few German aircraft crashing in the area and a few bombs being dropped near Cleobury Town (Walltown Farm) the line and depot remained unscathed throughout the war, only being forced to close, and then not through enemy action, in the hard winter of 1947, when the whole village was cut off. Mr Ivan Cartwright and other local R.N.A.D. employees were set to work clearing snow off the roads.

The frenzied activity on the branch continued throughout the duration, and No. 29 assisted at times by No. 2001 were kept busy, No. 28 also occasionally being seen with, from 1944 0-6-0PT No. 2044 whilst No. 29 was away for short spells at Hereford. The heavily loaded ammunition trains they dealt with were brought to Cleobury Junction by a varied assortment of locomotives including LNER 'J25' 0-6-0s on wartime loan to the GWR, 'Aberdares', and 'Dean Goods', whilst the heaviest engines recorded on the Ditton Priors sidings at Cleobury Mortimer were '28XX' 2-8-0s; another type, 'Bulldog' 4-4-0 No. 3393 *Australia* was noted in the Bayton Colliery sidings, hauling out a train of ammunition vans.

Every inch of space on the branch was used for storage, even Cleobury Town engine shed, unused since 1938 was commandeered as an ammunition store, women being brought by road every day from Ditton Priors to work cleaning shell cases in the old fitters cabin.

With the coming of peace the hectic pace on the branch slowed down. The needs of the depot meant reverting to the pre-war practice of coming from Kidderminster but running through only as far as a new exchange siding, well outside the R.N.A.D. security fence near Cleobury North.

Here the wagons were exchanged with the R.N.A.D. loco which had made the short journey from Ditton Priors over GWR metals. Facilities for the watering of GW locos were provided just south of the exchange sidings in the shape of a stand pipe operated by a large wheel.

No. 29 charges up Hatton Bank on a running-in trip from Stafford Road Works in 1945.

V.R. Webster

In November 1945 No. 28 was sent to Swindon for much needed repairs, followed a while later in 1947 by No. 29 which stayed there on loan during the final days of the GWR's existence, returning to Kidderminster in time to pass on to its new owners, the British Transport Commission.

After Nationalisation the line came under the Western Region of the new British Railways, and although no immediate changes were to be made affecting the line, the first thing the new owners did was to send No. 28 to Hereford on loan in April 1948, following which it returned to Kidderminster via a short stay at Worcester where it was given a new chimney. No. 29 on the other hand was given a special treat in having a new cowl fitted at Worcester in October of the same year.

Lack of employment meant that No. 28 was placed in open store at Kidderminster in 1949 followed by a spell, again in store, at Gloucester in June 1950. Eventually No. 28 was brought into use once more, being loaned to the Hafod N.C.B. Colliery, Wrexham, for shunting their sidings. From there it was sent to Swindon via Kidderminster again for another period of storage, in September 1951. For most of this time No. 29 had remained in active work on the branch.

Attention was once more paid to the condition of the permanent way and in 1950-51 some work was done on replacing lengths of track on the branch, one small stretch had concrete sleepers laid as an experiment. The track which crossed the road at Detton Ford and carried wagons beneath the loading bins was lifted, the ropeway pylons and all other metalwork having been removed for scrap during the war.

Kidderminster shed was given the BR code 85D in February 1950 and it was at this time that 0-6-0 No. 2101 was on loan and then permanently allocated to share the branch work with others of the same class, Nos. 2051 and 2093. No. 29, still at Kidderminster, now made only occasional trips up the branch often driven by Mr Bill Breakwell (by now the last ex-CM & DP footplateman) but used more frequently as Kidderminster yard shunter or for boiler washouts at its home shed.

No. 29 still remained active at the time in 1953 when its sister, No. 28 (then at Newport, Dock Street), was condemned but lingered on only a couple of months into 1954 when No. 29 went to Swindon via Worcester. Whilst at Worcester it made its stay memorable by falling into the traverser pit at the works. At this time the GWR figures "29" were still clearly visible on the front

Cleobury North exchange sidings in 1965.

K. Beddoes

and rear buffer beams but, like No. 28, no smokebox number nor shedplate had been fitted. The "death" of 28 and 29 were mourned in the columns of *Trains Illustrated* and an article appeared comparing their power to the '2021' class. Although this was the end of the ex CM & DP locos Lord Boyne's estate was still remembered by the name on ex-GWR Hall No. 6932 *Burwarton Hall* which had been built in 1941 when No. 29 ex-*Burwarton* had been struggling with the war effort.

Early in 1954, 0-6-0PT No. 2101 and another of the '2021' class No. 2144, were in control of the branch freight but when 2101 was transferred to the LM Region, 0-6-0PT No. 2034 came at first on loan from Worcester (85A) and then was ultimately allocated to Kidderminster (85D) in April 1954, inheriting No. 29's cowl in the process.

Freight services on the branch were now run "as required", usually one, but sometimes as many as three trips per week. The Admiralty intimated, however, that they considered the depot to be of some lasting importance which caused the operating staff of BR something of a problem because the remaining locos of the '2021' class were, at this time, being condemned in some numbers and very few were available locally as replacements. The only other classes light enough for use on the branch were 0-6-0s of the '1361' classes or the relatively new Hawksworth designed but BR built '16XX' class. One of this type No. 1629 was at Worcester already fitted with a cowl for shunting the Vinegar Works siding and it was decided to try it on the branch from 21st July, 1954 for a week or so. It was an immediate success and well suited to the work because soon after this trial a sister engine No. 1661 arrived "dead" at Kidderminster delivered brand new from Swindon works in March 1955. It was set to work immediately and replaced No. 2034, special instructions being issued that locos of the '16XX' class were not to run over the passing loops on the branch with the exception of those at Cleobury North transfer sidings.

Soon after No. 1661 arrived the branch enjoyed the sight of passenger traffic again with scenes reminiscent of the passenger closure day in 1938. The occasion was the Stephenson Locomotive Society's West Midland Branch line tour which was hauled into Cleobury Mortimer behind 0-6-0 Dean Goods No. 2516 (now preserved); '2021' class No. 2144 (by then allocated to 85A) then took charge of the four coach train, the first bogie passenger stock ever to take the branch curve out of the Junction. The train journeyed up the branch as far as Cleobury

North transfer sidings before returning to the Junction. This historic run was to be 2144's "swan song" for she was withdrawn just a week later.

0-6-0PT No. 1629 had another brief spell on the branch in mid 1957 whilst No. 1661 was away at Gloucester but No. 1661 was back on hand to work the last BR hauled train in September 1957.

It was still not yet the end for the CM & DP branch. The line was not to close to traffic at all but was destined to revert to its original independent existence. As long as two years previously in December 1955, a British Transport Commission Bill provided for the take over of the whole branch by the Admiralty at a cost to them of £40,000 and they eventually came to own the line from 1st May, 1957 and began operating the route from 30th September, 1957 having first purchased a standard 20 ton BR brake van which the Admiralty repainted off white.

The motive power available was two Ruston and Hornsby 165 hp 0-4-0 diesel mechanical shunters, which had been delivered to Ditton Priors for the munitions transfer traffic in 1950 replacing an older 4W DM No. 99. The new Ruston Hornsbys were given "Ditton Priors Yard" Nos. 35 and 36 and were housed at Ditton Priors in a small brick shed which had been built by the Admiralty. The drivers of the diesels were Messrs Harry Hodnett and Noel Padgett who were accompanied for some weeks by BR drivers teaching them the route. Messrs Charlie Cartwright and Mr Harry Hall were shunter/guards. One permanent way gang looked after the length from Cleobury Mortimer to Stottesdon whilst a second gang maintained the area above Stottesdon to Ditton Priors. Members of the southern end's gang included Messrs Walter Caines, Charlie Carter, Walter Jones, Jim Tennant, Fred Nicholas, Jack Holton and Bill Watkiss. The other gang was made up from Messrs. Jack Duce, George Bennett, Bill Davis, Arnold and Mick Bounds. All of these men were employed by the Admiralty but were supervised by an inspector from BR.

The line was run under the same rules as the GWR and BR ('Sound horn at crossings' etc) but Cleobury Mortimer bound trains had to be brought to a stand at a "stop lamp" just up the branch (0m 21ch) from the Junction signal box, the guard obtaining a key from the signalman. This enabled him to open a ground frame catch point to give access to the BR station. The exchange traffic was then dealt with in Ditton Priors sidings. As this traffic dwindled in the early sixties it was obvious that in this

Although of poor quality, this rare photograph taken in September 1946 shows No. 28 (left) and No. 29 together at Kidderminster shed, both sporting spark arresting chimneys. Hand rail differences may be noted.
P.F. Curtis

With Driver Jack Bacon in charge, No. 29 passes by the old CM & DP headquarters at Cleobury Town on its way to Cleobury North for Admiralty traffic on 18th September, 1952. Guard Ted Teague stands on the brake van verandah.

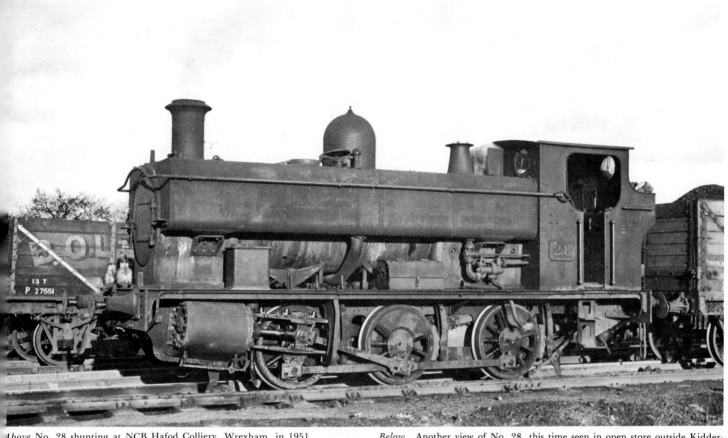

Above No. 28 shunting at NCB Hafod Colliery, Wrexham, in 1951.

Below Another view of No. 28, this time seen in open store outside Kidderminster shed in the same year.

Above　0-6-0PT No. 2051 at Kidderminster in 1951.

R.S. Carpenter

Below　0-6-0PT No. 2034 on 19th April, 1954, at Kidderminster. Although allocated to 85D, the locomotive still carries 85A shed plate.

M. Hal

Right No. 29 passes over Cleobury North Crossing on 18th September, 1952.

G.F. Bannister

Below On 23rd February, 1954, 0-6-0PT No. 2144 heads a freight northwards just past Wyre Crossing.

G.F. Bannister

Above 0-6-0PT No. 2101 is in charge of a freight at Aston Botterell on 16th April, 1953.

G.F. Bannister

Below Also on 16th April, 1953, the same locomotive passes Prescott Siding the head of a Ditton Priors bound freight.

G.F. Bannist

At Kidderminster on 2nd June, 1957, was 0-6-0PT No. 1661.   *M. Hale*

and many other rural areas, rail traffic had only a short life in front of it, threatened by the policy of abandonment being carried out by Lord Beeching.

The through passenger service from Kidderminster to Woofferton Junction ceased on 31st July, 1961 followed by the consequent experimental truncated service to Tenbury Wells closing a year later leaving only the "Tenbury Goods" as a link down the Wyre Forest line. This situation remained until Tenbury Wells station was closed in January 1964. Kidderminster shed closed in the same year, engines working to Cleobury Mortimer with Ditton Priors transfer traffic now being supplied by Stourbridge Shed.

It came as no real surprise in the district when the Admiralty announced that its depot at Ditton Priors was to finish operation in the early part of 1965 for the sole traffic into the Junction now was run "as required by the Admiralty".

Traffic on the CM & DP branch finally ceased on Good Friday 16th April, 1965 and from May electric token working from Bewdley North Box to Cleobury Mortimer was withdrawn which meant that the whole Tenbury branch was then worked as a siding.

Some Admiralty equipment was allowed to be moved out by rail which delayed the intended lifting of the Cleobury-Bewdley section of the Tenbury line, but by the end of June the depot

had finally closed and the diesels had been transported away on low loader road vehicles.

Whilst demolition of the Tenbury-Cleobury section had been in progress a group of local railway enthusiasts were actively trying to preserve something of South Shropshire's railways and a tentative enquiry was made to the Admiralty about the possibility of the CM & DP being sold. A rough figure of £12,000 was given which was very cheap compared to today's inflationary prices, as preservationists well know. However, the many restrictions imposed on the working of the branch plus the impending rail isolation caused the group to drop their idea and pursue their original aim of preserving part of the Severn Valley line.

In November of that year lifting began between Cleobury and Bewdley and once again a scheme was voiced to save the CM & DP branch but after considering all the pitfalls the promoter changed his mind, the line then being left to drift into obscurity.

The Naval Depot at Ditton Priors after closure had been maintained by a small security staff under the charge of Mr Dick Glaze and Mr. H. Morris until February 1967 when a contingent of the U.S. Army came from France to set up a temporary ammunition dump. There was speculation from rail enthusiasts at least that the line would come into use again borne out of a local newspaper column on 19th February, which read:

Closed rail line may be reopened to serve the new American Army base at Ditton Priors. Details of the possible reopening were first given by the Secretary of State for Defence when he answered a Commons question by Mr Jasper More, the local M.P. for Ludlow at the time. Mr. More said the roads in the Ditton Priors area were inadequate for the volume of trucks serving the base. The Secretary replied that any damage to the roads would be made good and that the implications of reopening the railway were being studied.

This last statement was farcical to say the least, for the same Ministry of Defence (which presumably would have run the line again) had already sold it and its fittings at the end of 1966 and all rail connection at the Cleobury Mortimer end had been lifted by BR. This meant any ammunition bound for Ditton Priors would have had to been off loaded from road vehicles at Cleobury Mortimer onto the light railway.

However this was not to be, for the Americans, with their big transport vehicles "improved" some of the local roads making them wide enough for Ditton Priors to be reached without hold ups or the need for the railway!

The Americans were at Ditton Priors nearly 18 months and towards the middle of their stay track lifting began. George Cohen Sons and Co. Ltd had the contract for this work from the Ministry of Defence. The removal of track at Ditton Priors was hindered by the fact that no burning equipment was allowed by the Americans inside the boundary fence and all rails there had to be patiently unbolted by hand and processed later outside the depot with a cutting torch. The track was lifted all down the line with the assistance of a Bucyrus 22 R.B crawler crane, a 955 trackbed shovel and a Jones K L 66 crane with a very small labour force compared with the huge contingent of railway navvies who had laid it all down sixty years previously.

The remnants of the branch were mostly sold locally except for a large consignment of wooden sleepers which went to a Doncaster firm and some of the rail which was used to reinforce sea defence walls on the North Sea coast.

The Americans departed from the depot in June 1968 and once more the depot was under the care of Mr Dick Glaze and Mr. Morris, until November 1971, when the Ministry of Defence disposed of its remaining assets, selling off the former R.N.A.D. buildings for the use of light industry.

The final act of severage had already taken place in 1969 when a team from the Army had blown up the brick bridge across the Bewdley-Cleobury road near Cleobury Mortimer Station, so closing the final chapter of the CM & DP.

The bridge over the Bewdley-Cleobury Mortimer road after demolition by the army in March 1969. Local legend stated that a pot of gold sovereigns had been bricked in when the bridge was built. However, no trace was found of the coins when the bridge was blown up.

Courtesy Shropshire Star

bove Dean Goods No. 2516 arrives at Cleobury Mortimer Junction with the
LS Branch Line Special on 21st May, 1955.   *Author*

Below No. 2144, displaying the express headlight code, halts at Cleobury
North platform for the fireman to open the gate.   *Author*

Above   No. 2144 replenishes its tanks at Kennel Crossing before running round its train at the exchange sidings and returning to Cleobury Junction with the SLS Special.

Below   Standing in the Ditton Priors platform at Cleobury Mortimer, No. 251 prepares to depart for Birmingham Snow Hill on 21st May, 1955.

R. V. Buckle

Above Heading north, No. 1661 nears Aston Botterell. Brown Clee Hills rise in the background.

G.F. Bannister

Below On 12th June, 1957, No. 1661 approaches Aston Botterell Siding.

G.F. Bannister

Above No. 1661 heads north through a wintry Shropshire landscape, with Titterstone Clee in the distance. 6th January, 1956.

G.F. Bannister

Below Admiralty diesel, Ditton Priors Yard No. 35 (Ruston & Hornsby class 165 DS), trundles into Cleobury Town.

A. Muckley

Above An Admiralty diesel draws past the catch points at Kennel Crossing near Cleobury North, ½ mile south of the boundary fence, in 1965.

Below Prescott Siding in Admiralty days.

A. Muckley

A. Muckley

Left 0-6-0PT No. 2019 ("850" class).
R.S. Carpenter Collection

Below 0-6-0PT No. 1629 in Worcester yard en route for store at Kidderminster shed on 26th June, 1960.

Brian Moone

Left A poor picture but the only one found showing 4W DM, Yard No. 99.

T. Davies Collection

CHAPTER ELEVEN

Postscript

THE route of the former CM & DP Lt Rly has begun to disappear into the landscape. However, memories of its very personal service remain. A service which could accommodate, for example, the unloading of a farmer's seed to the exact field by the lineside where it was required, or the regular stopping to pick up an elderly lady passenger from Goesland, where no station ever existed. Good pieces of steam coal were often thrown off in wartime to stoke the fires of soldiers camped out by their lineside searchlight; a farm horse which fell and stuck in the mud and was hauled out by a locomotive and rope; a train which was specially decorated for a local wedding party.

In the early days of the line Mr Ernie Wall of Oreton lived at Detton Mill as a young boy, and remembers some of the navvies sleeping rough in the mill, at the time of the construction. Many were from London and many did not go back, sometimes getting jobs on local farms. Some of the navvies did not bother with the provided accommodation and stayed in turf built shelters (like the one illustrated on p. 34). One such man remembered by Mr E. Wall, was William Wood, nicknamed "Darky" who cooked hedgehogs on an open fire, and washed himself daily in the River Rea! (The strength of these men has always been legendary, and Mr Wall can recall feats of weightlifting using massive flour bags when the navvies returned to the mill after a day's work often done for 4d (2p) per hour).

Mr Jim Lawley, of Cleobury Mortimer, remembers the cutting of the long earthworks from Cleobury Mortimer up to Wyre Crossing and beyond to Cleobury Town Station. He has been able to identify many of the personnel on one of the photographs of the Wilson steam navvy in use. The job of the wagon spragger, Mr Tom Dalloway, was to use a tip-cat (a prepared stick) which was poked through the wheel of a spoil truck thereby braking it and causing it to tip its load, whilst Mr Joe Lawley was rope runner and stood on the platform in front of the navvy below the bucket which traversed the boom, and tipped the bucket manually. Turpin Laws had been with Bott and Stennett on other contracts and had always played a large part in looking after many horses involved in the work.

Other memories exist. Bottles of home made cider passed to a thirsty driver at the height of summer with the bottle returned by a gentle lob from the cab on the faster return run down the gradient. Fur and feather of all kinds being gathered by chance or intention. Young BR drivers trying to beat the unofficial speed record down the line with a load of empties coming back from the depot at Ditton Priors. No. 2144, in a thunderstorm slithering to a stop on the 1 in 60 grades, taking over 2 hours to cover the 12 miles. The fireman who shovelled the token onto the fire by mistake and watched it melt. The guard who got left behind after seeing his train safely across a road crossing. The railway trolley used by a young boy to cart hay from a lineside field after the last train had been run and the trouble that followed for him with the management of the time. The games of quoits played in the waiting room at Ditton Priors.

It should be remembered too, what a good safety record the line had particularly with the many unguarded road crossings, each one a potential site of danger. There were just a few accidents on the crossings. Mr Frank Rudd was carried several hundred yards down the track in his small car at Burwarton crossing in 1948 but emerged unhurt. A van was bumped at Detton Ford crossing and a dozing farmer in pony and trap was given a sudden shock by an oncoming train at the same point. At Neen Lane crossing in 1928, Mr Whatmore was shot out of his open car following a collision but fortunately none of these were serious accidents or resulted in injury to the people concerned.

Needless to say the environment that the line grew up in has changed. Alternative materials giving better quality surfaces are used in place of dhustone which is nevertheless still quarried, and although the Magpie Quarry no longer functions, the Titterstone Clee is still the site of a large scale quarrying industry.

The May Fair at Ditton Priors with its large livestock auction did not survive the First World War and Cleobury Mortimer's weekly Wednesday market and annual sheep sale have gone. Stottesdon and Burwarton farmers can get convenient access to Bridgnorth or Kidderminster by road.

Seventy years after construction the track bed has, in many places, been ploughed back out of existence. Cleobury Town yard is still used as a store for materials, the concrete post and panel houses and the crossing gates are still there too. The engine shed is battered but still standing and the one time existence of the flat rail bed is noticeable at most of the old road crossings. Burwarton station waiting room and porter's room still stands used as a shelter by livestock. The various bridges across the Rea are in good condition still and the brickwork admired years ago by Mr Walter Atkinson is there to see. At Ditton Priors, much of the station site is taken over for building though plenty remains of the R.N.A.D. days including their ex BR brake van body in use at present as a chicken shed, and part of the security fence still serves that purpose but now enclosing the "Blists Hill" open air museum near Ironbridge and at least one part of the line is preserved, namely the parachute tank from Cleobury Town, now residing at the Chacewater Railway near Cannock. The route of the Abdon Clee inclined railway has been concreted over in part and many of the remains of the buildings shown on the map are still clearly traceable on the top of Abdon Burf.

The passenger service came late and went early compared to many other British railways. It could never be said that this side of the enterprise was an economic success but it did provide an amenity over its thirty years operation in a rural area.

The line was built for the purpose of transporting dhustone but once the supply of rock from the Abdon area of the Brown Clee began to falter it was very difficult for the railway to diversify its goods traffic. The siting of the R.N.A.D. depot provided an unexpected prolongation of life for the branch but the "panniers with a spark arrester" as they ran in this period are what many people associate with the "Gadget". There are many "ifs" to conjure with, as with all railways, including the advantages of a possible extension to a junction with the Wenlock branch or the link with Billingsley Colliery. Neither happened but in any case the Edwardian railway age that produced the original idea of this Light railway has been gone a long time.

Above left The parachute tank at Cleobury Town station.

K. Beddoes

Top right The Ditton Priors branch platform disappearing beneath the undergrowth at Cleobury Mortimer Junction in 1974.

W. Smith

Above The engine shed at Cleobury Town, roofless and derelict in 1974.

W. Smith

Left The remains of Burwarton station in 1974.

W. Smith

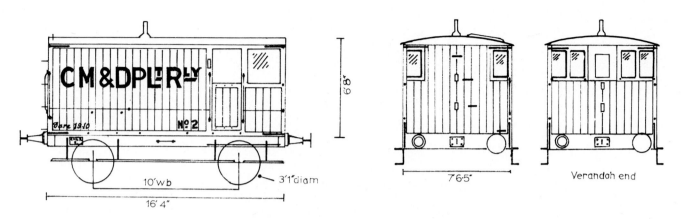

20 ton goods brake van, Cleobury Mortimer & Ditton Priors Light Railway No. 2.

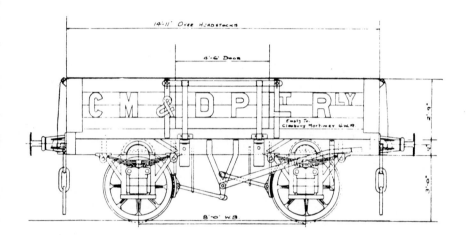

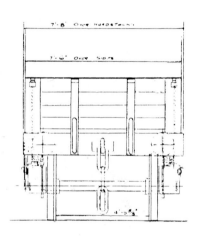

Cleobury Mortimer & Ditton Priors Light Railway 8 ton goods wagon.

Courtesy K. Werrett

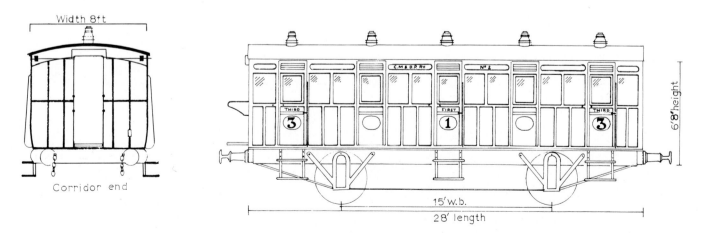

CM & DP 1st/3rd class composite coach No. 2, previously running on the North London Railway.

Left An illustration of a Motor Rail petrol vehicle No. 969, identical to Nos. 848 and 1029 used at Abdon Clee. L./Corporal D. Canham sits at the controls in France, 1918.

Courtesy Mrs. M.A. Smith

Below Diagram of a 2 ft gauge Motor Rail "whizzbang" used by the Abdon Clee Quarry Company on the line serving the crushing plant.

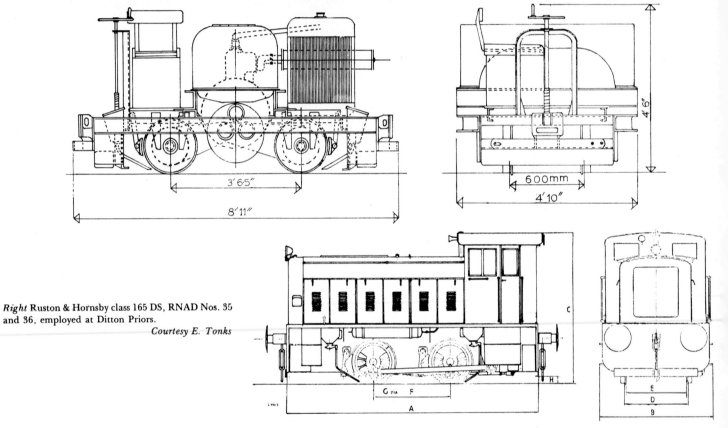

Right Ruston & Hornsby class 165 DS, RNAD Nos. 35 and 36, employed at Ditton Priors.

Courtesy E. Tonks

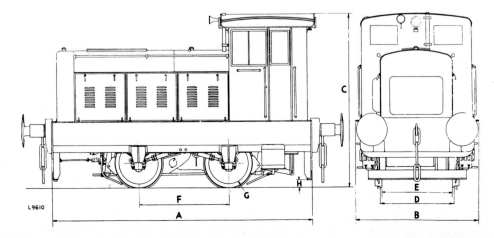

Left Ruston & Hornsby class 88DS, RNAD No. 99 also used on the Ditton Priors branch.

Courtesy E. Tonks

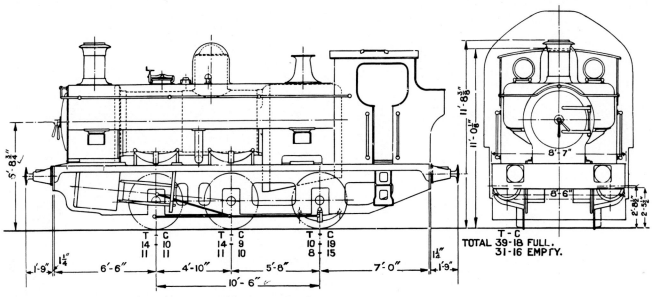

Above Diagram of rebuilt CM & DP locomotive (GWR No. 28). Detail differences between Nos. 28 and 29 included handrails, tank vents, tank balance pipes and bunker beading.

OPC/British Rail

Below Diagram of CM & DP loco No. 1735 as built.

Courtesy D. Townsley

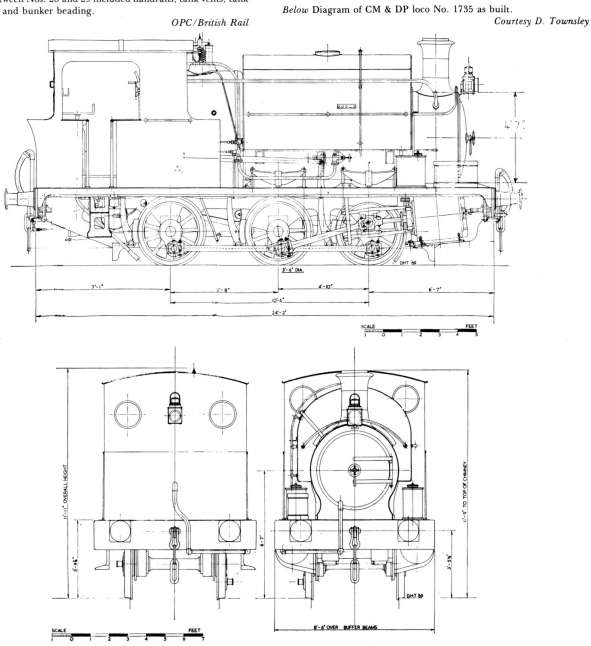

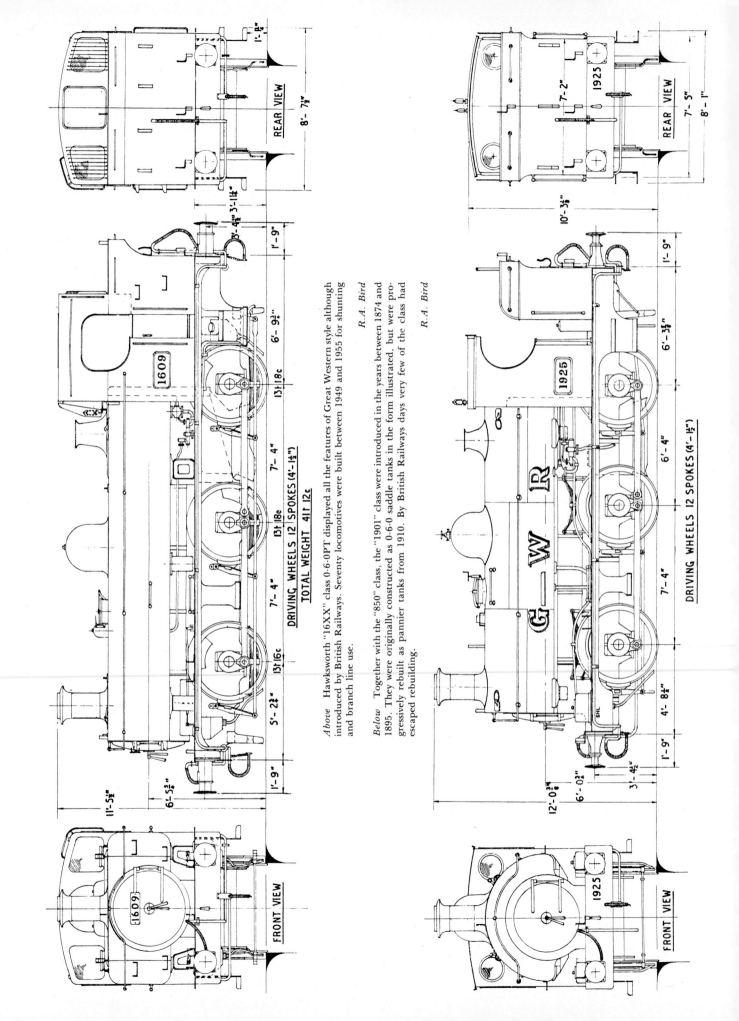

REAR VIEW

1609

REAR VIEW

1925

Above Hawksworth "16XX" class 0-6-0PT displayed all the features of Great Western style although introduced by British Railways. Seventy locomotives were built between 1949 and 1955 for shunting and branch line use.

R.A. Bird

Below Together with the "850" class, the "1901" class were introduced in the years between 1874 and 1895. They were originally constructed as 0-6-0 saddle tanks in the form illustrated, but were progressively rebuilt as pannier tanks from 1910. By British Railways days very few of the class had escaped rebuilding.

R.A. Bird

DRIVING WHEELS 12 SPOKES (4'-1½")
TOTAL WEIGHT 41t 12c

DRIVING WHEELS 12 SPOKES (4'-1½")

FRONT VIEW

1609

FRONT VIEW

1925

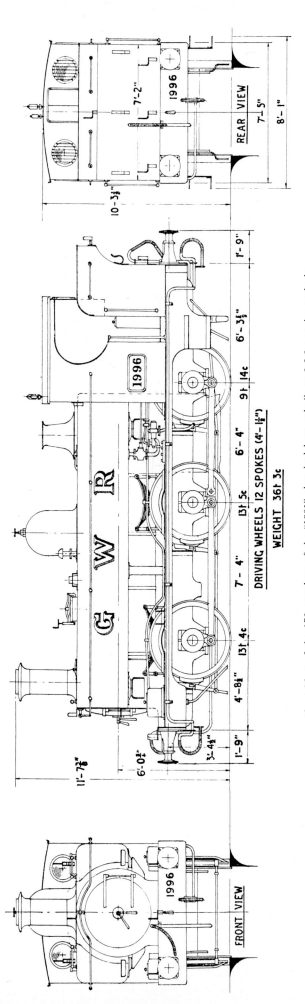

DRIVING WHEELS 12 SPOKES (4'-1½")

WEIGHT 36t 3c

Above Most of the 170 members of the "1901" class had been rebuilt as 0-6-0 pannier tanks by Nationalisation, and No. 1996, of Lot X2 delivered in 1891, is shown in this form.

R.A. Bird

Below Like the "1901" class, the "2021" class were originally designed as 0-6-0 saddle tanks and subsequently rebuilt as pannier tanks. The first member of the class was introduced in 1897.

R.A. Bird

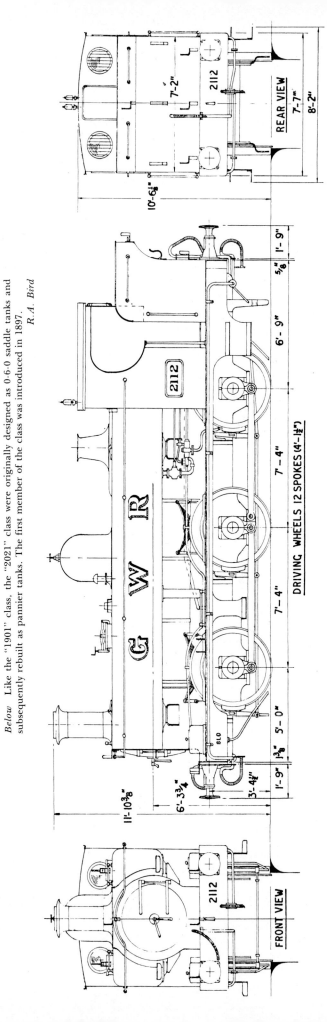

DRIVING WHEELS 12 SPOKES (4'-1½")

CLEOBURY MORTIMER AND DITTON PRIORS BRANCH.

SINGLE LINE.—Worked by Train Staff.   No Block Telegraph.—Only one Engine in Steam or two Engines coupled together allowed on this Branch at the same time.

Mile Post Mileage.	STATIONS.	Ruling Gradient.	Time allowances Point to Point times for Freight Trains.	DOWN TRAINS.—WEEK DAYS ONLY.						Goods. arr. P.M.	Goods. dep. P.M.					
M C	**Cleobury Mortimer**	—	Minutes.	..	....	..	....	..	..	—	2 30	..	....	....	..	..
1 38½	*Wyre Common Crossing	60 R	—	....	....	....	....	...	..			....		..	..
1 78½	§Cleobury Town Halt	60 R	12	..	..	..	....	..	..	2 43	2 48	....	..	..	..
2 18½	*Neen Lane Crossing	100 F	—	..	....	...	..	...	..			....	..	..	..
2 68½	*Chilton Siding & Crossing	100 F	6	..	....	....	....	...	...	—	2 55	..	....	...	..
4 26	*Detton Ford Sdg. & Cros.	60 R	9	..	....	....	....	..	..	3 5	3 8	..	..	...	..
5 25½	*Prescott Siding & Crossing	88 R	6	....	....	..	....	....	..	3 15	3 18	..	....	....	..
5 55½	*Old Lane Crossing	88 R	—	....	....	....	....	..	..			....	..	....	..
5 75½	*Day House Crossing	88 R	—	....	....	....	....	..	..			....	..	..	..
6 58½	*Stottesdon Station & Cros.	66 R	9	..	..	..	....	..	..	3 28	3 33	..	..	....	..
8 45	*Aston Botterell Sdg.&Cros.	60 R	11	..	....	..	..	..	...	3 45	3 48	..	..	..	..
9 25½	*Burwarton Station & Cros.	60 R	5	....	....	....	..	..	..	3 54	3 59	....	..	....	..
10 38	§Cleobury N. Plat. & Cros.	60 R	7	..	..	..	....	..	..	4 7	R4 10	..	..	..	..
10 58	*Kennel Crossing ..	60 R	—	....	....	..	....	..	..			....	..	..	..
11 75½	**Ditton Priors**	60R to level	9	..	..	..	..	..	..	4 20	—	..	....	..	..

	STATIONS.	Ruling Gradient.	Time allowances Point to Point times for Freight Trains.	UP TRAINS.—WEEK DAYS ONLY.					Goods. arr. P.M.	Goods. dep. P.M.					
		level to 60 F	Minutes.	..	..	..	..	..	—	4 35	..	..	..	..	..
	Ditton Priors	60 F	—	..	....	..	....	....	4 40	P4 42	....	..	....	..	..
	Stop Board	60 F	—	..	....	...	....	...			....	...	..	..	..
	*Kennel Crossing ..	60 F	—	..	..	..	....	....	4 48	R4 51	....	..	..	..	..
	§Cleobury N. Plat. & Cros.	60 F	9	..	..	..	....	...	4 59	5 4	....	..	..	..	..
	*Burwarton Station & Cros.	60 F	7	..	....	..	....	..	C R		..	....	....	..	..
	*Aston Botterell Sdg.&Cros.	60 F	5	..	....	..	....	..	5 21	5 26	..	..	..	..	..
	*Stottesdon Station & Cros.	66 R	11	..	..	...	..	..	—	—	....	..	..	..	..
	*Day House Crossing	88 R	—	..	....	..	....	..	C R		..	....	..	..	..
	*Old Lane Crossing	88 R	—	..	..	..	..	..			....	..	..	..	..
	*Prescott Siding & Crossing	88 F	9	..	....	..	....	..	5 43	5 48	..	..	..	..	..
	*Detton Ford Sdg. & Cros.	60 F	6	..	....	..	..	..	C R		..	....	..	..	..
	*Chilton Siding & Crossing	100 R	9	..	....	..	....	..			....	..	....	..	..
	*Neen Lane Crossing ..	100 R	—	..	..	..	..	..	6 4	6 9	..	..	..	..	..
	§Cleobury Town Halt	60 F	6	..	....	..	....	..			....	..	..	..	..
	*Wyre Common Crossing	60 F	—	..	....	..	....	..			....	..	..	..	..
	Stop Board	60 F	4	..	....	..	....	..	6 14	P6 16	..	..	..	..	..
	Cleobury Mortimer	60 F	9	..	..	..	..	..	6 26	—	..	..	..	..	..

R Trainmen to open and close Gates at Cleobury North Crossing.

*Intermediate Public Crossings without gates but provided with Cattle Guards.

§ Public Level Crossing with gates.

———

SPEED RESTRICTIONS.

No train or engine must exceed a speed of 10 miles per hour at any point on the Branch, and speed must be further reduced to 5 miles per hour round curve approaching Cleobury Mortimer Station.

Note:—A speed indication board (not illuminated) is provided at a distance of about 300 yards on either side of the Public Road Level Crossings which are not provided with gates.

Cleobury Mortimer & Ditton Priors branch working timetable, issued in 1939.

126   No. 12.

MAXIMUM LOADS FOR ENGINES ON CLEOBURY MORTIMER AND DITTON PRIORS BRANCH.

SECTION. From	To	Engine No. 28 or 29 or 2100 Class. Class of Traffic. 1	2	3	Empties.	Engines of 1901 Class. Class of Traffic. 1	2	3	Empties.
Cleo. Mortimer Jct.	Cleobury Mortimer	12	14	18	24	11	13	17	22
Cleobury Mortimer	Detton Ford	21	25	32	42	20	24	30	40
Detton Ford	Ditton Priors	12	14	18	24	11	13	17	22
Ditton Priors	Detton Ford	21	25	32	42	20	24	30	40
Detton Ford	Cleobury Mortimer	17	20	26	34	16	19	24	32
Cleobury Mortimer	Cleo. Mortimer Jct.	19	23	29	38	18	22	27	36

Table indicating maximum permissible loads for the branch.

RIFLE RANGE HALT.
(Between Kidderminster and Bewdley).

Halt lamps to be trimmed, cleaned and lighted by Bewdley Porter, and extinguished by Guard working last trip.

Bewdley, Loop Siding.

This Siding, which runs parallel with the Back Road Single Line, must be considered as a Traffic Siding only, and not as a Running Loop Line. Shunting operations must not be conducted at both ends of the Siding at the same time.

CLEOBURY MORTIMER.
Bayton Colliery Company's Private Siding.

The connection to these Sidings is from the Great Western Sidings at the Neen Sollars end of Cleobury Mortimer Yard.

The traffic to and from these Sidings is dealt with by Great Western Engines, Guards and Shunters.

An Engine "Stop Board" is fixed in the Bayton Company's Sidings 112 yards from the Boundary Gate, beyond which no Engine must pass.

The Colliery Company's weighbridge and Coal Shoots are situated beyond the Engine "Stop Board" and Great Western Guards and Shunters are responsible for seeing that the Shoots are raised before propelling any vehicle past them.

Catch Points for the protection of Great Western Sidings are situated two yards on the Great Western side of the Boundary Gate.

Assisting Goods Trains out from Cleobury Mortimer to the Up Starting Signal.

The Scheduled Maximum Load for Goods Trains as between Cleobury Mortimer and Neen Sollars may be exceeded from Cleobury Mortimer whenever there is an Engine available to assist the Train out of the latter Station.

Shunting at Cleobury Mortimer.

Shunters, Guards and other persons doing work at Cleobury Mortimer are requested to bear in mind that the space is narrow between the rails and the girders of the bridge carrying the line over the road at the Bewdley end of the platforms, and there is not sufficient room for anyone to stand on the bridge whilst trains or vehicles are passing over it. No vehicles must be coupled up or uncoupled on the bridge.

In all cases when shunting operations are carried on at the Bewdley end of the Station, the engine must be on the Bewdley side of the vehicles.

The following Engine Whistles are in use in connection with the shunting operations at Cleobury Mortimer:—

From Loop or Yard to Colliery ... 4 Whistles.
From Loop or Yard to Spur ... 3 ,,
From Loop or Yard to Main Line ... 2 ,,

Cleobury Mortimer—Goods Loop.

The Goods Loop at Cleobury Mortimer cannot always be kept clear of station traffic, and Drivers of Trains entering the Loop should keep a careful look out to avoid coming too sharply into contact with traffic standing therein.

CLEOBURY MORTIMER AND DITTON PRIORS BRANCH.

The Line is a single one from Cleobury Mortimer to Ditton Priors, about 12 miles long; it is worked by Train Staff—without Train Tickets or Block Telegraph—in accordance with the instructions in the General Appendix to the Book of Rules and Regulations for working Single Lines of Railway by one engine in steam, or two or more engines coupled together.

CLEOBURY MORTIMER AND DITTON PRIORS BRANCH—continued.

Side Lamps are not carried on trains working over this Branch.

Prescott and Aston Botterell Sidings.

Vehicles must only be picked up or put off at these Sidings by Down Trains.

Shunting at Detton Ford.

Shunting at Ditton Priors.

Speed Restrictions.

Public Road Level Crossings.

CLEOBURY MORTIMER AND DITTON PRIORS BRANCH.

Public Road Level Crossings.

Neen Lane Crossing 2m. 18½c. between Cleobury Town and Stottesdon.

Prescott and Aston Botterell Sidings.

Crossing Gates at Cleobury Town and Cleobury North Crossings.

Fog Signalling, etc., Arrangements.

Shunting at Ditton Priors.

A red peg is provided in the Abdon Clee Stone Quarries Company's Sidings to indicate the point beyond which engines must not pass.

Cleobury Mortimer and Ditton Priors Branch—continued.
Engine Whistles.

Occupation of the Cleobury Mortimer and Ditton Priors Branch by Engineering Department.

BROMYARD BRANCH.
Freight Trains.

Suckley.
Down Freight Trains.

Brockhampton and Stream Hall Sidings.

Movement of Locos to and from Kidderminster Shed (KDR) to work CM & DP Branch
1927–1938

Loco No	From	Date	To	Notes
2101	WOS	18.5.27	Cleobury	Whilst No. 28 away for tubes
29	KDR	18.10.27	WOS Factory	
29	WOS Factory	18.11.27	KDR	
2101	KDR	19.11.27	WOS	
28	KDR	8.2.28	SDN	With tools off 1962
1962	KDR	8.2.28	Cleobury	With tools off 28
29	KDR	2.2.29	WOS Factory	
2019	WOS	9.2.29	Cleobury	
28	KDR	31.8.29	SDN	Via WOS
2019	WOS	6.9.29	Cleobury	
2019	KDR	9.9.29	WOS	Hot Box at Cleobury M.
29	Cleobury	13.12.29	WOS	Wheel Truing and Attention to Coupling
2051	WOS	7.2.30	Cleobury	
29	WOS	22.2.30	KDR	From WOS Factory
28	KDR	1.9.30	SDN	For Rebuild
2001	WOS	1.9.30	Cleobury	To Replace No. 28
2101	WOS	1.12.30	KDR	To Replace No. 28
803	SDN	12.2.31	KDR	To Replace No. 28
2101	KDR	21.2.31	WOS	
2001	KDR	3.3.31	WOS	
1220	WOS	6.4.31	Cleobury	To Replace 803 (Failed)
1220	KDR	11.4.31	WOS	
803	KDR	3.9.31	WOS	With tools off 2197
2197	SDN	1.9.31	KDR	
28	SDN	1.12.31	KDR	Returned Rebuilt
29	KDR	1.2.31	SDN	Repairs
29	SDN	20.2.32	KDR	
2197	KDR	22.2.32	NEA	Via WOS to Neath
28	KDR	14.8.33	WOS	
28	WOS	23.8.33	KDR	From WOS Shops
29	KDR	20.11.33	WOS	To WOS Factory
29	WOS	9.12.33	KDR	From WOS Factory
28	KDR	21.12.33	WOS	To WOS Factory
28	WOS	2.5.34	KDR	From WOS Factory
29	KDR	9.1.35	WOS	
29	TYS	23.1.35	KDR	
28	KDR	25.2.35	WOS	
28	WOS	27.3.35	KDR	From WOS Factory
29	KDR	15.7.35	WOS	To WOS Factory
28	KDR	28.8.35	WOS	To WOS Factory Hot Box
28	WOS	31.8.35	KDR	
29	WOS	7.10.35	KDR	From WOS Factory
29	KDR	1.6.36	WOS	To WOS Factory
2001	WOS	1.6.36	KDR	
29	WOS	6.6.36	KDR	From WOS Factory
28	KDR	10.6.36	WOS	To WOS Factory
28	WOS	7.8.36	KDR	From WOS Factory
2001	KDR	3.9.36	WOS	
29	KDR	4.12.36	WOS	To WOS Factory
2001	WOS	8.12.36	KDR	
2001	KDR	11.12.36	WOS	
2001	WOS	19.12.36	KDR	
2001	KDR	24.12.36	WOS	
2001	WOS	31.12.36	KDR	
2001	KDR	2.1.37	WOS	
29	WOS	15.1.37	KDR	From WOS Factory
29	KDR	23.9.37	SRD	To SRD Factory
29	KDR	17.11.37	WOS	To WOS Factory
1220	WOS	29.11.37	KDR	
1220	KDR	21.12.37	WOS	
29	SRD	26.1.38	KDR	From SRD Factory
2001	KDR	27.1.38		
28	KDR	19.4.38	WOS	To WOS Factory
2001	WOS	19.5.38	KDR	
28	WOS	17.8.38	KDR	From WOS Factory
2001	KDR	17.8.38	WOS	
29	KDR	27.9.38	WOS	Stopped for Repairs

Details of GWR Four Wheeled Stock used on the Branch throughout the period 1922–1938

GWR No.	Built	Lot	Diagram	Description
4263/4	c.1880		N.L.R.	28′0″ x 8′0″ W.B. 15′0″ Brake 3rd
6342/3	c.1880		N.L.R.	28′0″ x 8′0″ W.B. 15′0″ 1x1st, 4x3rd
954	1901	978	T.36	31′0¾″ x 8′0¾″ Brake 3rd
6482	1891	586	U.4	26′10″ x 8′0¾″ Composite
6308	1902	990	U.4	26′10″ x 8′0¾″ Composite
2657	1895	738	T.34	31′0¾″ x 8′0¾″ Brake 3rd

Comparison of traffic on CM & DP based on yearly reports for 1913 and 1920

Passengers	1913	1920
1st Class	189	36
3rd Class	13,353	11,048
Goods		
Merchandise	1,333 tons	6,757 tons
Coal, coke & Patent Fuel	5,582 tons	7,216 tons
Other minerals	121,045 tons	99,264 tons
Livestock	2,688 animals	1,130 animals
Principal classes of Merchandise carried		
Roadstone	117,769 tons	98,483 tons
Grain	56 tons	504 tons
Cattle	323	121
Calves	31	1
Sheep	2,196	985
Pigs	138	23
Timber	86 tons	1,299 tons
Iron & Steel bars/plates	nil	174 tons
Girders, billets & ingots	nil	—
Scrap iron	25 tons	79 tons
Hay & Straw	91 tons	—
Fruit & Vegetables	60 tons	—
Manure	—	717 tons
Sand	—	20 tons

Details of Engines which worked CM & DP Branch in numerical order (1922–1957)

GW/BR No	Class	Built/Rebuilt	Withdrawn	Spark Arrester
28	Ex CMDPR	Reb. 1930/1	11.53	†R
29	Ex CMDPR	Reb. 1924	2.54	Y
803	Ex LMMR	1911	3.51	N
1220	850	1877	11.38	N
1629	1600	1950	6.60	Y
1948	850	1887	8.34	N
1661	1600	1955	7.64	Y
1970	850	1890	7.38	N
1962	850	1889	2.29	N
2001	850	1891	8.52	Y
2019	850	1895	12.49	N
2034	2021	1897	9.55*	Y
2044	2021	1898	7.51	Y
2051	2021	1898	7.51	Y
2093	2021	1903	1.52	Y
2101	2021	1902	3.56	Y
2144	2021	1904	5.55	Y
2197	Ex BPGVR	1909	10.52	N

* Sold to N.C.B. Sept 1955. Caerphilly Tar Works to end of 1958. At Hafody-Ryny Colliery May 1961. Then at N.C.B. Blaenavon. Scrapped March 1964.
† R = Rare, Y = Yes, N = No.

The Light Railway Commission.

MAY, 1907.

STOTTESDON, KINLET & BILLINGSLEY
LIGHT RAILWAY.

ESTIMATE OF EXPENSE.

Railway No. 1.

		Miles	fur.	chs.		Whether Single or Double.
Length of Line		5	2	1		Single.
Gauge, 4ft. 8½ins.						

Earthworks:	Cubic yds.	Price per yd.			£ s. d.
		s.	d.	£ s. d.	
Cuttings—Rock ...	...	...		...	
Soft Soil ...	85,000	1	3	5,312 10 0	
Roads ...	...	...		...	
TOTAL ...	85,000	......		5,312 10 0	5,312 10 0

Embankments, including Roads ...	...	...	Cubic yards, Nil		—
Bridges—Public Road	...	...	Number—1		750 0 0
Railway and River ...	...	...	Number—Nil		—
Accommodation Bridges and Works ...	...	...	...		250 0 0
Culverts and Drains	...	...	...		2,000 0 0
Metallings of Roads and Level Crossings	...	...	...		500 0 0
Gatekeepers' Houses at Level Crossings	...	...	Nil.		—

Permanent Way, including Fencing:—					
	Miles	fur.	chs.	Cost per mile.	
	5	2	1	@ £1,600 0s. 0d.	8,420 0 0
Permanent Way for Sidings, and Cost of Junctions	...	...	...		100 0 0
Stations	...	...	...		750 0 0
					£18,082 10 0
Contingencies	...	...	10 per cent.		1,808 5 0
		A.	R.	P.	
Land and Buildings	...	35	0	0	875 0 0
				TOTAL	£20,765 15 0

STOTTESDON, KINLET & BILLINGSLEY
LIGHT RAILWAY.

ESTIMATE OF EXPENSE.

SUMMARY.

		Length.				Cost.	
		M.	F.	C.		£ s. d.	
Railway No. 1		5	2	1		20,765 15 0	
Railway No. 2		0	2	8		2,910 0 0	
Railway No. 3		0	2	0		2,029 7 6	
Total length ...		5	6	9	Total cost	£25,705 2 6	

Dated this 31st day of May, 1907.

WILLIAM T. FOXLEE,

Engineer.

Above Estimate of expense for the construction of the Stottesdon, Kinlet & Billingsley Light Railway.

Left Estimate of expense summary for the construction of the three sections of the Stottesdon, Kinlet & Billingsley Light Railway.

Below Proposed route of the SK & BLR, with an enlargement showing the layout at the Billingsley Colliery terminus.

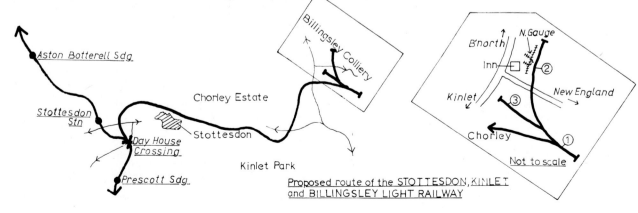

Proposed route of the STOTTESDON, KINLET and BILLINGSLEY LIGHT RAILWAY

SUMMARY OF WAGON ROLLING STOCK ABSORBED BY GWR FROM CM & DP LT. RLY.

Type	CM & DP No	GWR No	Matl	Body Details Length	Body Details Width	HT	Frame Matl	W.B.	Bearing Spring Length	Journals	Wheel No + Diam	Axle Boxes	Buffers	Draw Gear	Brakes	Tare	Load	Built Date	Built Lot	Renumbering Date	Condemned Date	Notes
Open Goods	1	34238	Wood	14'7½"	7'0"	2'4"	Wood	9'0"	3'6"	8x3¾"	4x3'1"	O/K	—	Cradle	Single	5.9.2	10T	1908	—	26.5.23 (NA)	11.6.27 (SDN)	Ellis A/Boxes Changed 5/23
"	2	34241	"	"	"	"	"	"	"	"	"	Ellis	—	Gedge & Cradle	"	5.14.3	"	"	"	30.12.22 (WOS)	5.9.25 (SDN)	—
"	3	34243	"	"	"	"	Oak	"	"	"	"	O/K	—	"	"	5.12.0	"	"	Brit Wag Co	6.10.25 (WOS)	3.9.27 (SDN)	—
"	4	34245	"	14'6½"	"	"	Wood	"	"	"	"	O/K	23x2½"	"	"	5.10.0	"	"	"	9.2.24 (SDN)	5.9.25 (SDN)	—
"	5	34246	"	"	"	"	Oak	"	"	"	"	O/K	—	"	"	5.15.0	"	"	"	15.8.23 (WOS)	11.6.27 (SDN)	—
"	6	34252	"	"	"	"	Wood	"	"	"	"	O/K	—	"	"	5.12.3	"	"	"	9.6.23 (SDN)	10.7.26 (SDN)	Were Ellis A/Boxes
"	7	34256	"	"	"	"	"	"	"	"	"	Ellis	—	Gedge & Cradle	"	5.13.0	"	"	"	31.1.23 (WOS)	27.10.28 (SDN)	—
"	8	34257	"	14'7"	"	"	"	"	"	"	"	O/K	—	Cradle	"	5.12.0	"	"	"	21.4.23 (WOS)	18.2.28 (SDN)	Were Ellis A/Boxes
"	9	34258	"	"	"	"	"	"	"	"	"	O/K	"	"	"	5.11.0	"	"	"	5.5.23 (WOS)	27.11.26 (SDN)	"
"	10	34263	"	14'6"	"	"	"	"	"	"	"	O/K	"	"	"		"	"	"	21.4.23 (WOS)	18.4.25 (SDN)	"
"	11	34268	"	14'7½"	6'11½"	"	"	8'0"	3'2"	7x3 7/16"	4x3'0"	O/K	SC	"	"	4.16.0	8T	1912	Conv B.W.C.	16.6.23 (SDN)	27.12.24 (SDN)	Changed to 10T 8/23
"	12	No wagon carrying this number at date of absorption																				
"	13	34269	—	—	—	—	—	—	—	—	—	—	—	—	—	—	—	1912	Conv B.W.C.	—	14.6.24	Not renumbered
"	14	34270	—	—	—	—	—	—	—	—	—	—	—	—	—	—	—	1912	"	—	22.4.23	"
"	15	34272	—	—	—	—	—	—	—	—	—	—	—	—	—	—	—	1912	"	—	31.12.22	"
"	16	34275	—	—	—	—	—	—	—	—	—	—	—	—	—	—	—	1912	Conv B.W.C.	—	24.3.23	Not renumbered
"	17	34277	—	—	—	—	—	—	—	—	—	—	—	—	—	—	—	"	"	—	24.3.23	"
"	18	34279	Wood	14'7"	6'11"	2'4"	Wood	8'0"	3'2"	7x3½"	4x3'0"	O/K	SC	Cradle	Single	4.15.0	8T	"	"	18.3.23 (SDN)	17.4.26 (SDN)	
"	19	34280	—	—	—	—	—	—	—	—	—	—	—	—	—	—	—	"	"	—	10.9.22	Not renumbered
"	20	34282	—	—	—	—	—	—	—	—	—	—	—	—	—	—	—	"	"	—	24.3.23	"
Covered	—	34283	—	—	—	—	—	—	—	—	—	—	—	—	—	—	—	"	"	—	8.10.22	"
Goods B.V.	1	10109	Wood	16'4"	7'6½"	6'8"	Wood	10'0"	4'0"	10x5"	4x3'1"	CMPD 10x5"	—	Gedge & Cradle	Screw	19.0.0	—		Glos C and WCo	31.1.23 (WOS)	27.6.36 (SDN)	Last survivor of Ex CMDP rolling stock
"	2	10110	"	—	—	—	—	"	—	"	"	"	—	Hook	8 blocks	19.5.0	—	—	—	3.2.23 (WOS)	24.9.32 (SDN)	

The CM & DP Lt Rly also had a 5 ton travelling crane plus match truck but no record has yet been found of this.
Note: Renumbering dates usually (but not always) week ending date.
Withdrawal date usually four weeks ending date.